D0044249

TO THE READER

Dianetics (from Greek *dia* "through," and *nous* "soul") delineates fundamental principles of the mind and spirit. Through the application of these discoveries, it became apparent that Dianetics dealt with a beingness that defied time—the human spirit—originally denominated the "I" and subsequently the "thetan." From there, Mr. Hubbard continued his research, eventually mapping the path to full spiritual freedom for the individual.

Dianetics is a forerunner and substudy of Scientology which, as practiced by the Church, addresses only the "thetan" (spirit), which is senior to the body, and its relationship to and effects on the body.

This book is presented in its original form and is part of L. Ron Hubbard's religious literature and works and is not a statement of claims made by the author, publisher or any Church of Scientology. It is a record of Mr. Hubbard's observations and research into life and the nature of man.

Neither Dianetics nor Scientology is offered as, nor professes to be physical healing, nor is any claim made to that effect. The Church does not accept individuals who desire treatment of physical or mental illness but, instead, requires a competent medical examination for physical conditions, by qualified specialists, before addressing their spiritual cause.

The Hubbard® Electrometer, or E-Meter, is a religious artifact used in the Church. The E-Meter, by itself, does nothing and is only used by ministers and ministers-in-training, qualified in its use, to help parishioners locate the source of spiritual travail.

The attainment of the benefits and goals of Dianetics and Scientology requires each individual's dedicated participation, as only through one's own efforts can they be achieved.

We hope reading this book is the first step of a personal voyage of discovery into this new and vital world religion.

This Book Belongs To

_____

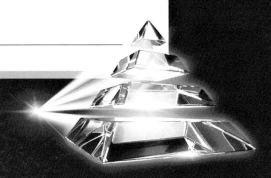

Dianetics
THE ORIGINAL THESIS

Dianetics
THE ORIGINAL THESIS

L. RON HUBBARD

Bridge
Publications, Inc.

A
HUBBARD®
PUBLICATION

Bridge Publications, Inc.
4751 Fountain Avenue
Los Angeles, California 90029

ISBN 978-1-4031-4486-7

© 2007 L. Ron Hubbard Library.
Artwork: © 2007 L. Ron Hubbard Library.
All Rights Reserved.

Any unauthorized copying, translation, duplication, importation or
distribution, in whole or in part, by any means, including electronic
copying, storage or transmission, is a violation of applicable laws.

*Book One, L. Ron Hubbard, Saint Hill, The Bridge, LRH,
Dianetica, Dianetics, Hubbard, OT, Purification, E-Meter*
and *Scientology* are trademarks and service marks
owned by Religious Technology Center
and are used with its permission.

Scientologist is a collective membership mark designating
members of the affiliated churches and missions of Scientology.

Bridge Publications, Inc. is a registered trademark and service mark in
California and it is owned by Bridge Publications, Inc.

NEW ERA is a trademark and service mark.

Printed in the United States of America

Important Note

In reading this book, be very certain you never go past a word you do not fully understand. The only reason a person gives up a study or becomes confused or unable to learn is because he or she has gone past a word that was not understood.

The confusion or inability to grasp or learn comes AFTER a word the person did not have defined and understood. It may not only be the new and unusual words you have to look up. Some commonly used words can often be misdefined and so cause confusion.

This datum about not going past an undefined word is the most important fact in the whole subject of study. Every subject you have taken up and abandoned had its words which you failed to get defined.

Therefore, in studying this book be very, very certain you never go past a word you do not fully understand. If the material becomes confusing or you can't seem to grasp it, there will be a word just earlier that you have not understood. Don't go any further, but go back to BEFORE you got into trouble, find the misunderstood word and get it defined.

Glossaries

In writing *Dianetics: The Original Thesis,* L. Ron Hubbard provided a glossary of all technical terms, defined as they are used in this book and in the sequence they should be learned. As such, the *LRH Glossary* forms a vital component of this text to be studied in full for a thorough comprehension of the nomenclature and subject itself.

To further aid reader comprehension, LRH directed the editors to provide definitions for other words and phrases. These are included in the Appendix, *Editor's Glossary of Words, Terms and Phrases.* Words sometimes have several meanings. The *Editor's Glossary* only contains the definitions of words as they are used in this text. Other definitions can be found in standard language or Dianetics and Scientology dictionaries.

If you find any other words you do not know, look them up in a good dictionary.

Foreword

D*ianetics: The Modern Science of Mental Health* is the most widely read book ever written on the human mind. More than half a century since original publication, it still rides bestseller lists in virtually every country of Earth and so fuels a movement now spanning the globe. For all those reasons and more, millions the world over refer to it simply as "Book One."

But in reality, the *first* book of Dianetics is the one you now hold in your hands. Originally written for the medical community, on whose patients Ron had developed and tested his discoveries, it was titled *Abnormal Dianetics* for the fact that it revealed the single source of all abnormal and irrational behavior. The book was not offered for official publication. Rather, copies of the original typewritten manuscript were circulated in limited numbers to a few select friends. The response was dramatic. Readers began copying the text themselves and further circulating it to friends. Those people, in turn, began doing the same. And so it continued until the groundswell of interest and letters requesting more information was so great they could only be answered with a book. That book was, of course, *Dianetics: The Modern Science of Mental Health*.

Yet for everything contained in Book One, the primary discoveries and basic equations at the foundation of all Dianetics encompasses today are contained herein. It was for this reason L. Ron Hubbard saw to its permanent publication with a first 1951 edition, renaming it with a self-explanatory title: *Dianetics: The Original Thesis*.

Of course, discoveries have been amplified by further discoveries and auditing procedures have evolved and been refined through continuing development. Nevertheless, this is still the book Ron referred to throughout the years as essential to an understanding of *how* and *why* auditing works.

Through exhaustive research, the original manuscript was recently discovered, containing Ron's previously unknown, handwritten edits. Also discovered were two entire chapters of the book—*The Analyzer* and *The Clear*—never previously published and yet providing the first description of the analytical mind and basic personality.

In reference to his *Original Thesis,* Ron once remarked, "It's got everything in it." Accordingly, so now do *you,* with the first complete and fully accurate publication of his original work.

It is with great pride we present *Dianetics: The Original Thesis.*

— The Editors

Contents

Introduction

In 1932 an investigation was undertaken to determine the *Dynamic Principle of Existence* in a workable form which might lead to the resolution of some of the problems of Mankind. A long research in ancient and modern philosophy culminated, in 1938, in the heuristically discovered Primary Law. A work was written at that time which embraced Man and his activities. In the following years, further research was undertaken in order to prove or disprove the axioms so established.

Certain experiences during the war made it necessary for the writer to resolve the work into applicable equations and an intensive program was begun in 1945 toward this end.

A year later many techniques had been discovered or evolved and a nebulous form of the present refined work was formulated. Financed chiefly by a lump sum disability compensation, that form of Dianetics was intensively applied to volunteer subjects and the work gradually developed to its present form.

Dianetics has been under test by the writer, as here delineated, for the past four years. The last series of random volunteers (numbering twenty) were rehabilitated, twenty out of twenty, with an average number of work hours of fifty-two per subject. Dianetics has been found to successfully resolve migraine headaches, ulcers, arthritis, astigmatism, bursitis, stammering, glandular imbalance, asthma, allergies and other psychosomatic ills. It has also successfully removed any compulsions, repressions, neuroses and psychoses to which it has been applied.

L. RON HUBBARD
1948

1

Part I

Discoveries and Principles
DIANETICS: THE ORIGINAL THESIS

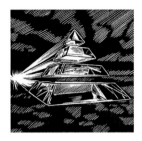

Chapter One
PRIMARY AXIOMS

Primary Axioms

D ianetics is a heuristic science built upon *axioms*. Workability rather than Truth has been consulted. The only claim made for these axioms is that by their use certain definite and predictable results can be obtained.

The principal achievement of Dianetics lies in its organization. Almost any of its parts can be found somewhere in history, even when they were independently evolved by the writer. There are no principal sources and where a practice or a principle is borrowed from some past school, the connection is usually accidental and does not admit any further use or validity of that school. Dianetics will work, and can only be worked, when regarded and used as a unity. When diluted by broader applications of older practices, it will no longer produce results. To avoid confusion and prevent semantic difficulties, new and simplified terminology has been used and is used only as defined herein.

Dianetics is actually a family of sciences. It is here addressed in the form of a science of thought applicable to *psychosomatic* ills and individual *aberrations*.

The field of thought may be divided into two areas which have been classified as the Knowable and the Unknowable. We are here concerned only with the Knowable. In the Unknowable we place that data which we do not need to know in order to solve the problem of improving or curing of aberrations of the human mind.

By thus splitting the broad field of thought, we need not now concern ourselves with such indefinites as spiritualism, deism, telepathy, clairvoyance or, for instance, the human soul.

Conceiving this split as a line drawn through the area, we can assign a *Dynamic Principle of Existence* to all that data remaining in the Knowable field. After exhaustive research, one word was selected as embracing the finite universe as a Dynamic Principle of Existence. This word can be used as a guide or a measuring stick and by it can be evaluated much information. It is therefore our first and our controlling axiom.

The first axiom is:

SURVIVE!

This can be seen to be the lowest common denominator of the finite universe. It embraces the conservation of energy and all forms of energy. It further delineates the purpose of that energy so far as it is now viewable by us in the Knowable field. The activity of the finite universe can easily be seen to obey this axiom as though it were a command. All works and energies can be considered to be motivated by it. The various kingdoms have this as their lowest common denominator, for animals, vegetables and minerals are all striving for survival. We do not know to what *end* we are surviving. And in our field of the Knowable and in our choice of only the workable axioms, we do not know and have no immediate reason to ask *why*.

All forms of energy are, then, surviving to some unknown end for some unknown purpose. We need only to know that they *are* surviving and that, as units or species, they *must* survive.

By derivation from the first workable axiom, we come into possession of the second. In obedience to the command "Survive!" life took on the form of a cell which, joining with other cells, formed a colony. The cell, by procreating, expanded the colony. The colony, by procreating, formed other colonies. Colonies of different types united and necessity, mutation and natural selection brought about specializing which increased the complexity of the colonies until they became an aggregation. The problems of the colonial aggregation were those of food, protection and procreation. In various ways, a colonial aggregation of cells became a standardized unity and any advanced colonial aggregation came into possession, by necessity, mutation and natural selection, of a central control system.

The purpose of the colonial aggregation was to survive. To do this it had to have food, means of defense, protection and means of procreation. The control center which had developed had as its primary command "Survive!" Its prime purpose was the food, defense, protection and means of procreation.

Thus can be stated the second workable axiom:

THE PURPOSE OF THE MIND IS TO SOLVE PROBLEMS RELATING TO SURVIVAL.

The ultimate success of the organism, its species or life would be, at its unimaginable extreme, immortality. The final failure in obedience to the law "Survive!" would be death. Between eternal survival and death lie innumerable gradations. In the middle ground of such a scale would be mere existence without hope of much success and without fear of failure. Below this point would lie, step by step, innumerable small errors, accidents, losses, each one of which would tend to abbreviate the chances of reaching the ultimate goal. Above this point would lie the small successes, appreciations and triumphs which would tend to secure the desirable goal.

As an axiom, the mind can then be said to act in obedience to a central basic command—"Survive!"—to direct or manage the organism in its efforts to accomplish the ultimate goal for the individual or species or life and to avoid for the individual or species or life any part of the final failure, which leads to the stated axiom:

THE MIND DIRECTS THE ORGANISM, THE SPECIES, ITS SYMBIOTES* OR LIFE IN THE EFFORT OF SURVIVAL.

---

*The Dianetic meaning of *symbiote* is extended beyond the dictionary definition, "the living together of two dissimilar organisms," to mean any or all life or energy forms which are mutually dependent for survival. The atom depends on the universe, the universe on the atom.

A study of the field of evolution will indicate that survival has been, will be and is the sole test of an organism, whether the organism is treated in the form of daily activity or the life of the species. No action of the organism will be found to lie without the field of survival, for the organism is acting within its environment upon information received or retained, and error or failure does not alter the fact that its basic impulse was motivated by survival.

Another axiom may then be formulated as follows:

THE MIND, AS THE CENTRAL DIRECTION SYSTEM OF THE BODY, POSES, PERCEIVES AND RESOLVES PROBLEMS OF SURVIVAL AND DIRECTS OR FAILS TO DIRECT THEIR EXECUTION.

As there are many organisms in the same species all attempting to accomplish the same end and as there are many species and as matter itself is attempting in one unit form or another to survive, there is necessarily conflict and contest among the individuals of the species, other species or units of matter. Species cannot survive without being interested primarily in the species. Natural selection and other causes have established this as a primary rule for survival: *That the unit remain alive as long as possible as a unit and, by association and procreation, that the species remain alive as a species.* Second-grade interest is paid by the unit or the species to its symbiotes. Third-grade interest is paid to inanimate matter. As this is apparently the most workable solution, natural selection best preserves those species which follow this working rule and the symbiotes of the successful species therefore have enhanced opportunity for survival.

Man is the most successful organism currently in existence, at least on this planet. Man is currently winning in the perpetual cosmic election which possibly may select the thinker of the New Thought.

Man is heir to the experience and construction of his own ancestors. As cellular conservatism is one of the factors of survival, his mind is basically the same mind which directed and resolved the problems of his animal forebears. By evolution and natural selection, this mind therefore has the primary priority in emergencies. Superimposed on this animal mind has been developed an enormously complex analyzer, which probably exists as his frontal lobe.

The command "Survive!" is variable in individuals and species to the extent that it may be strong or weak. Superior strength of the command in the individual or species is normally, but variably, a survival factor. The primary facet of personality is the basic strength of the *dynamic** drive.

The dynamic is variable from individual to individual and race to race. It is varied by physiology, environment and experience. Its manifestation in the animal mind affects both the tenacity of the individual to life or purpose and it affects the activity of the analyzer. The first characteristic of the individual which should be considered is the basic strength of his dynamic, by which an axiom can be formulated:

THE PERSISTENCY OF THE INDIVIDUAL IN LIFE IS DIRECTLY GOVERNED BY THE STRENGTH OF HIS BASIC DYNAMIC.

The analytical, human, or as it has elsewhere been called erroneously, the conscious mind, is variable from individual to individual and race to race in its ability to perceive and resolve problems. Another axiom can then be formulated:

INTELLIGENCE IS THE ABILITY OF AN INDIVIDUAL, GROUP OR RACE TO RESOLVE PROBLEMS RELATING TO SURVIVAL.

It should be noted that there is a distinct difference between the dynamic and the intelligence. High intelligence may not denote high dynamic. High dynamic may not denote high intelligence. Intelligence is mental sensitivity and analytical ability. Dynamic is the persistency of the individual in obedience to the command "Survive!"

---

*Dynamic: the dynamic thrust into time and space of an individual, a species, or a unit of matter or energy. Especially defined, for the purpose of Dianetics, as "Survive!"

"The persistency of the individual in life is directly governed by the strength of his basic dynamic."

It has been noted that there is a gradation in the scale of survival. Gains toward the ultimate goal are pleasurable. Failures toward the final defeat are sorrowful or painful. *Pleasure* is therefore the perception of well-being or an advance toward the ultimate goal. *Pain* therefore is the perception of a reduction toward the final defeat. Both are necessary survival factors.

For the purpose of Dianetics, good and evil must be defined.

Those things which may be classified as *good* by an individual are only those things which aid himself, his family, his group, his race, Mankind or life in its dynamic obedience to the command, modified by the observations of the individual, his family, his group, his race or life.

As *evil* may be classified those things which tend to limit the dynamic thrust of the individual, his family, his group, his race or life in general in the dynamic drive, also limited by the observation, the observer and his ability to observe.

Good may be defined as constructive. *Evil* may be defined as destructive. (Definitions modified by viewpoint.)

The individual man is an organism attempting to survive in affinity or contest with other men, races and the three kingdoms. His goal is survival for himself, his progeny, his group, his race, his symbiotes, life and the universe in general, in contest with any efforts or entities which threaten or impede his efforts to attain the goal. His happiness depends upon making, consolidating or contemplating gains toward his goal.

It is a purpose of Dianetics in general, and *Abnormal Dianetics* in particular, to pass Man across the abyss of irrational, solely reactive thought and enter him upon a new stage of constructive progression to the ultimate goal.

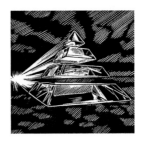

Chapter Two

An Analogy of the Mind

An Analogy of the Mind

I t is not the purpose of Abnormal Dianetics to investigate or accurately reconstruct the *human mind*. The purpose of Abnormal Dianetics is to delete from the existing mind those physically painful experiences which have resulted in the aberration of the analytical mind, to erase from the body psychosomatic illnesses which are physical abnormalities and the physical manifestation of the aberration, and to restore in its entirety the proper working function of a mind not otherwise physically deranged.

Abnormal Dianetics embraces the various physiological aspects of psychosomatic medicine, including the glandular balance or imbalance of the organism as influenced by painful physical experiences.

The measurement and increase of the dynamic is the practice and study of Dynamic Dianetics, which subject is not included in this manual. The initial adjustments of the individual are included in Child Dianetics and Educational Dianetics. Surgical and medical procedures as they affect the mind are covered in Medical Dianetics, which is briefly touched upon in this manual. Judicial Dianetics, Political Dianetics and Military Dianetics are elsewhere touched upon or allocated for study. Dianetics as a family of sciences proceeds, however, from the axioms cursorily touched upon in the last chapter and is uniformly governed by the principles of the behavior of the human mind as enhanced by the techniques of Abnormal Dianetics.

All human activity proceeds primarily from the impulses covered in the primary science, Dynamic Dianetics, which deals as above with the basic dynamic, its measurement and enhancement. The existence and variability of this dynamic are not primarily a subject for Abnormal Dianetics, but must be considered as the only primary thrust in obedience to which the mind and body react.

When the individual is acting contrary to the survival of himself, his group, progeny, race, Mankind or life, he can be considered to be unintelligent, uninformed or aberrated. *Every single instance of aberrated conduct threatening the general goal of the individual, as outlined in the last chapter, can be proven to have a source which will specifically be found to be a painful experience containing data not available to the analytical mind.* Every single instance and facet of aberrated conduct has its exact causation in the physically painful error which has been introduced during a moment of absence of the analytical power.

Abnormal Dianetics consists of discovering the aberration in the individual, finding the physically painful experience which corresponds to it and deleting the perceptic content of that experience from the body and mind.

More as an effort to demonstrate how that is accomplished than as an actual outline of the character of the mind, the following analogy is offered.

First there is the *physio-animal* section of the mind. This contains the motor controls, the sub-brains and the physical nervous system in general, including the physical aspect of the analytical section of the mind. The control of all voluntary and involuntary muscles is contained in this section. It commands all body fluids, blood flow, respiration, glandular secretion, cellular construction and the activity of various parts of the body. Experimentation has adequately demonstrated this. The physio-animal mind has specific methods of "thinking." These are entirely reactive. Animal experimentation—rats, dogs, etc.—is experimentation on and with precisely this mind and little more. *It is a fully conscious mind and should never be nominated by any term which denies it "consciousness," since there is no period in the life of the organism from conception to death when this mind is not awake, observing and recording perceptions.* This is the mind of a dog, cat or rat and is also the basic mind of a man, so far as its operating characteristics are concerned. A man in the deepest possible somnambulistic sleep is still in possession of more mind and thinking and coordinating ability than a lower animal.

The term "consciousness" is no more than a designation of the awareness of "now." The physio-animal mind never ceases to be aware of now and never ceases to record the successive instances of now, which in their composite make up a *time track* which connects memory in an orderly chain. Cessation of life alone discontinues the continual recording of perceptions on this orderly track. "Unconsciousness" is a condition wherein the organism is dis-coordinated only in its analytical process and motor control direction. In the physio-animal section of the mind, a complete time track and a complete memory record of all perceptions for all moments of the organism's existence is available.

As life progresses, for instance, from a blade of grass to a dog, greater and greater complexities and degrees of self-determinism are possible. Energy in its various forms is the primary motivator in the lower orders. But as the complexity of the order is increased into the animal kingdom, the physio-animal mind attains more and more command of the entire organism until it itself begins to possess the second section of the mind.

All animals possess, in some slight degree, an analyzer. This, which we designate the *analytical mind,* is present even in lower orders, since it is only that section of the mind which possesses the self-deterministic coordinative command of the physio-animal mind and thus of the body. In a rat, for instance, it is no more than its "conscious" awareness of *now* applying to lessons of *then,* without rationality, but with instinct and painful experience. This is the analytical section of the mind in a lower animal, but it is the *reactive mind* in a man, whose analytical mind is so highly attuned and intricate that it can command entirely both the physio-animal mind and thus the body.

Man not only possesses a superior physio-animal mind, but possesses as well an analytical mind of such power and complexity that it possesses no real rival in any other species. The analytical mind of Man cannot be studied by observing the reactions of animals under any situations. Not only is it more sensitive, but it possesses factors and sensitivities not elsewhere found.

Continuing this analogy, lying between the analytical mind and the physio-animal mind may be conceived the *reactive mind*. This is the coordinated responses of the physio-animal mind, the "analytical" mind of animals and the first post of emergency command in Man. All errors of a psychic or psychosomatic nature can be considered, for the purposes of this analogy, to lie in the reactive mind. The first human analytical mind took command of the body and physio-animal mind under strained and dangerous circumstances when Man was still in violent contest with other species around him. It can be considered that the analytical mind received command with the single proviso that instantaneous emergency would be handled by the outdated, but faster, reactive mind.

Any and all errors in thinking and action derive from the reactive mind as it is increased in strength and power by painful experience. It can be called a "shadow mind," instantaneously reactive when any of its content is perceived in the environment of the individual, at which time it urgently bypasses the analytical mind and causes immediate reaction in the physio-animal mind and in the body. Additionally, the reactive mind is in continual presence when chronically restimulated by a constantly present *restimulator*—which is to say, an approximation of the reactive mind's content or some part thereof continually perceived in the environment of the organism. The reactive mind is in action so long as it is activated by an exact or nearly exact approximation of its content. But given too continuous a restimulation, it can and does derange both the physio-animal mind and body below it and the analytical mind above it. It was created by deranging circumstances of a physical nature, hence it deranges.

"Continuing this analogy, lying between the analytical mind and the physio-animal mind may be conceived the reactive mind."

The entire content of the reactive mind is records of physical pain with its accompanying perceptions during disconnection of the analyzer. All aberrated conduct and error on the part of an individual is occasioned by restimulation of his reactive mind.

None of these minds are "unconscious," nor are they "subconscious." The entire organism is always conscious. But the temporary dispersion of the thought processes of the analytical mind brings about a condition whereby that mind, having been dispersed and considering itself the residence of person, is unable to obtain and reach data perceived and received by the organism during the analytical mind's condition of dispersion. That the analytical mind can be thrown, by pain or shock, out of circuit is a survival factor of its own: as sensitive "machinery" it must be protected by a fuse system.

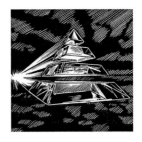

Chapter Three
The Dynamics

The Dynamics

The *basic dynamic*—"Survive!"—increases in complexity as the complexity of the organism evolves. Energy may be considered to have taken many paths through eternity to arrive intact at the infinite goal. The *why* of the goal may lie above the finite line. But below it—demarked by the word "Survive!"—definite manifestations are visible. Energy collects into various forms of matter, which collect and aggregate in various materials and compounds. Life evolves from the simplest basic into complex forms, since evolutionary change is in itself a method of survival.

Conflict among species and individuals within the species is additionally a survival factor. Affinity of individuals for groups, races and the whole of its species and for other species is additionally a survival factor, as strong or stronger than conflict.

Dynamic is defined as the dynamic thrust through time toward the attainment of the goal. "Survive!" is considered to be the lowest common denominator of all energy efforts and all forms.

It can then be subdivided specifically into several dynamic lines as applicable to each form or species. The unaberrated self contains four main dynamics* which are held in common with Man.

The dynamics are: One, *personal;* Two, *sex;* Three, *group;* and Four, *Mankind.*

An entire philosophy can be built around each one of these dynamics which will account for all the actions of an individual. Any one of these philosophies is so complete that it can be logically made to include the other four. In other words, all purpose of an individual can be rationalized into the personal dynamic. A philosophy exists which attempts to rationalize everything into the sexual dynamic. And so on, with all the dynamics. Observing that each one can stand as a logical unity, one finds it necessary to retire to the lowest common denominator of the basic dynamic which actually does explain the four subdivisions. As each one of the subdivisions is capable of supporting the whole weight of a rational argument, it can readily be deduced that each is of nearly equal importance in the individual. The aberrated conditions of a society tend to vary the stress on these dynamics, making first one and then another the keynote of the society. In an unaberrated individual or society, the validity of all four would be recognized.

The unaberrated individual may physiologically possess or environmentally stress one or more of these dynamics above the others. In terms of *basic personality,* as covered in the field of Dynamic Dianetics, the physiological-environmental-educational aspect of the individual is varied in strength in the four dynamics.

Each one of the four dynamics breaks further into purposes which are specific and complex. Purposes and other factors entangle these dynamics and varying situations and the observational power of the individual may conflict one against another of these dynamics within the individual himself. This is a basic complex factor of the unaberrated personality.

---

*The four dynamics are not new forces; they are subdivisions of the basic dynamic.

I. The PERSONAL DYNAMIC consists of the dynamic thrust to survive as an individual, to obtain pleasure as an individual and to avoid pain. It covers the general field of food, clothing and shelter, personal ambition and general individual purpose.

II. The SEXUAL DYNAMIC embraces the procreation of progeny, the care of that progeny and the securing for that progeny of better survival conditions and abilities in the future.

III. The GROUP DYNAMIC embraces the various units of the species Man, such as the association, the military company, the people in the surrounding countryside, the nation and the race. It is characterized by activity on the part of the individual to obtain and maintain the survival of the group of which he is a part.

IV. The MANKIND DYNAMIC embraces the survival of the species.

While Man is concerned with any one of the above dynamics, any one of them may become antipathetic to his own survival. This is *rational conflict* and is normally and commonly incident to survival. It is non-aberrative in that it is rational within the educative limitation.

The family as a unit is not a dynamic, but a combination of dynamics. And in this and other societies, it attains a position of interest which is not necessarily inherent in the individual or group.

Basically simple, complexity is introduced among the dynamics by individual and group irrationalities. The basic (unaberrated) individual has continual difficulty rationalizing the problems of importances and choices among these dynamics. When the basic individual becomes aberrated and is attendantly unable to reason freely on all problems, a selection of importances among these dynamics becomes nearly impossible and produces aberrated solutions which may resolve such an extreme as the destruction of the individual himself, by himself, under the mistaken solution that he may thus obey the primary command.

Note: All self-destructive effort is irrationality of a precise nature which will often be found by the *auditor** in a person under treatment, but which forms no part of the basic personality of the individual.

---

*The term *auditor* is used in Dianetics to designate someone skilled in the practice of Dianetic therapy, called *auditing*. (The conduct of an auditor is covered later.)

The Four Dynamics

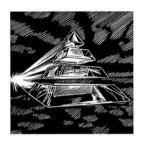

Chapter Four

The Basic Individual

The Basic Individual

For the purposes of this work, the terms *basic individual* and *Clear* are nearly synonymous, since they denote the unaberrated self in complete integration and in a state of highest possible rationality. A *Clear* is one who has become the *basic individual* through therapy.

The precise personality of the basic individual is of interest to the auditor. His complete characteristic is established by:

1. The strength of his basic dynamic.

2. The relative strengths of his dynamics.

3. The sensitivity, which is to say, the intelligence of his analyzer.

4. The coordination of his motor controls.

5. His physiological and glandular condition.

6. His environment and education.

The experiences of each individual also create an individual composite and so may additionally designate individuality. There are as many distinct individuals on Earth as there are men, women and children.

That we can establish a common denominator of dynamic and basic function does not, cannot and will not alter the fact that individuals are amazingly varied one from the next.

It will be found by experience and exhaustive research, as it has been clinically established, that the basic individual is invariably responsive in all the dynamics and is essentially good. There are varying degrees of courage, but in the basic individual there is no pusillanimity. The virtues of the basic individual are innumerable. His intentional vices and destructive dramatizations are non-existent. He is cooperative, constructive and possessed of purpose. In short, he is in close alignment with that ideal which Mankind recognizes as an ideal. This is a necessary part of an auditor's working knowledge, since deviations from it denote the existence of aberration and such departures are unnatural and enforced and are no part of the self-determinism of the individual.

Man is not a reactive animal. He is capable of self-determinism. He has willpower. He ordinarily has high analytical ability. He is rational and he is happy and integrated only when he is his own basic personality.

The most desirable state in an individual is complete self-determinism. Such self-determinism may be altered and shaped to some degree by education and environment. But so long as the individual is not aberrated, he is in possession of self-determinism. So long as he is self-determined in his actions, he adjusts himself successfully to the degree that his environment will permit such an adjustment. He will be more forceful, effective and happier in that environment than when aberrated.

That the basic personality is good does not mean that he cannot be a terribly effective enemy of those things rationally recognizable as destructive to himself and to his.

The basic individual is not a buried, unknown or different person, but an intensity of all that is best and most able in the person. The basic individual equals the same person minus his pain and dramatizations.

"Man is not a reactive animal.
He is capable of self-determinism. He has willpower.
He ordinarily has high analytical ability.
He is rational and he is happy and integrated
only when he is his own basic personality."

The dynamic strength of the person does not derive from his aberrations. The aberrations lessen the dynamic strength. Artistry, personal force, personality, all are residual in the basic personality. This is derived from clinical research and experimentation. The only reason an *aberree* (aberrated individual) occasionally holds hard to his aberrations is because his *engrams* have a content which forbids their removal.

Chapter Five

ENGRAMS

Engrams

T he *reactive mind* consists of a collection of experiences received during an unanalytical moment which contains pain and actual or conceived antagonism to the survival of the individual. An *engram* is a perceptic entity which can be precisely defined. The aggregate of engrams compose the reactive mind.

A new sub-field entitled *perceptics* has been originated here to adequately define engramic data. Perceptics contains, as one of its facets, the field of semantics. Precisely as the field of semantics is organized, so is organized in perceptics each sensory perception.

The audio-syllabic communication system of Man has its counterpart in various languages observable in lower animals. Words are sounds in syllabic form, delivered with a definite timbre, pitch and volume or sight recognition in each case. Words are a highly specialized form of audio-perceptics. The quality of the sound uttering the word is nearly as important as the word itself. The written word belongs in part to visio-perceptics. Having but lately acquired his extensive vocabulary, the mind of Man is least adjusted to words and their sense. The mind is better able to differentiate among qualities of utterance than among the meanings of words themselves.

Included in perceptics, in the same fashion and on the same axioms as semantics, are the other sensory perceptions: organic sensation, the tactile sense, the olfactory sense and the senses involved with sight and hearing. Each has its own grouping.

And each carries its class of messages with highly complex meanings. Each one of these divisions of the senses is plotted in time, according to the earliest or most forceful significances. Each class of messages is so filed as to lead the individual toward pleasure and away from pain. The classifications and study of this varied sensory file have been designated *perceptics*.

When injury or illness supplants the analytical mind, producing what is commonly known as "unconsciousness," and when physical pain and antagonism to the survival of the organism are present, an *engram* is received by the individual. Subsequently, during moments when the potential of the analytical mind is reduced by weariness, illness or similar circumstances, one or more of the perceptics contained in the engram may be observed by the individual in his environment and, without his perceiving that he has observed it or the identity of it, the individual discovers himself in a *dramatization* of the moment of receipt of the engram.

An engram impedes one or more dynamics of the basic individual. Being antagonistic to his survival, it can be considered analogically to consist of a "reverse charge."

As an example, the analytical mind can be said to possess multiple scanners in layers. Ordinary or pleasurable memory can be considered to have, as an analogy only, a "positive charge." The multiple scanners are able to sweep these areas and make available memory data to the analytical mind so that it can arrive, by various mathematical means, at a solution for its various problems.

The engram, as a specific memory package, can be considered to have a "reverse charge" which cannot be reached by the scanners of the analytical mind, but which is directly connected to the motor controls and other physical functions and which can exert (at a depth not nearly as basic as the basic dynamic, but nevertheless low) a hidden influence upon the analytical mind through another circuit. The analytical mind in awareness of "now" nevertheless is unable to discover (without therapeutic assistance) the existence of such an engram, since it was received during a moment of extremely low potential on the part of the analytical mind.

"During moments when the potential of the analytical mind is reduced by weariness, illness or similar circumstances, one or more of the perceptics contained in the engram may be observed by the individual in his environment and, without his perceiving that he has observed it or the identity of it, the individual discovers himself in a dramatization of the moment of receipt of the engram."

As a further analogy and for demonstration only, an engram can be considered to be a bundle of perceptions of a precise nature. An engram is an entire dramatic sequence implanted during unconsciousness which possesses specific perceptic keys, any one of which, when unanalytically perceived by the individual in his environment, may in greater or lesser degrees set the engram into reaction.

Denied to the analytical mind at its reception, it is denied to the analytical mind in its exact character during its dramatization. Its content is literal and, on the physio-animal level, demands action. Man's analytical ability and his vocabulary are imposed above both the physio-animal mind and the reactive mind, both on the evolutionary time track and in awareness. The charge contained in the engram is inexhaustible and remains reactive in full force whenever keyed into the circuit by restimulators.

Restimulators are those approximations in the environment of an individual of the content of an engram. Restimulators can exist in any of the various senses. The orderly filing of perceptics in the memory does not apparently include the content of engrams, these being filed separately under an "immediate danger" heading.

There are three kinds of *thought.* The first is *engramic,* or *literal.* It demands immediate action without examination by the analytical mind. A hand being withdrawn from a hot stove when burned is being governed by the reactive principle, but as the ensuing instant of unconsciousness caused by the shock is ordinarily slight, no real engram can be said to have formed.

The second type of thought is *justified thought.* Engramic thought is literal, without reason, irrational. Justified thought is the attempt of the analytical mind to explain the reactive, engramic reactions of the organism or the mind in the ordinary course of living. Every engram may cause some form of aberrated conduct on the part of the individual. Justified thought is the effort of the conscious mind to explain away that aberration without admitting, as it cannot do normally, that it has failed the organism.

The third and optimum type of thought is *rational thought*. This is the thought used by a Clear.

An engram is an apparent surcharge in the mental circuit with certain definite, finite content. That charge is not reached or examined by the analytical mind, but that charge is capable of acting as an independent command.

When the basic dynamic of the individual is boosted in potential by an observed necessity, the residual charge in engrams is insufficient to contest, at times, the raised purpose. The analytical mind can then be seen to function in entire command of the organism without serious modification by engramic command.

At other times, hostility in the environment and confusion of the analytical mind combine to reduce the dynamic potential to such a degree that the engramic command, in comparison to the basic dynamic, can be seen to be extremely powerful. It is at such times, in the presence of even faint restimulators, that the individual most demonstrates his aberrations.

An engram is severely painful or severely threatening to the survival of the organism and is an engram only if it cannot be reached by the awake analytical mind.

A simple approximation of the action of an engram can be accomplished by an experiment in hypnotism whereby a positive suggestion is delivered to an amnesia-tranced patient which contains a post-hypnotic signal. The subject, having been commanded to forget the suggestion when awake, will then perform the act. This suggestion is then actually a light portion of the reactive mind. It is literally interpreted, unquestioningly followed, since it is received during a period of unawareness by the analytical mind or some portion of it. The restimulator, which may be the act of the operator adjusting his tie, causes the subject to commit some act. The subject will then explain why he is doing what he is doing, no matter how illogical that action may be. The post-hypnotic suggestion is then recalled to the subject's mind and he remembers it. The compulsion vanishes (unless it is laid upon an actual engram).

The obedience of the subject to the command has as its source engramic thought. The explanation by the subject for his own action is the analytical mind observing the organism, which it supposes to have in its sole charge, and justifying itself. The release of the post-hypnotic suggestion into the analytical mind brings about rational thought.

Engrams can be considered to be painfully inflicted, often timeless, post-hypnotic suggestions delivered antagonistically to the "unconscious" subject. The post-hypnotic suggestion given the subject in the above example would not have any permanent effect on the subject, even if it were not removed by the operator, because there was presumed to be no antagonism involved (unless, of course, it rested on a former engram).

For every engram there is a *somatic* as part of that engram. No aberration exists without its somatics unless it is a racial-educational aberration, in which instance it is compatible with its environment and so is not considered irrational.

Every *aberration* contains its exact command in some engram.

The number of engrams per individual are relatively few. The aberrated condition of the individual does not depend on the number of engrams, but the severity of individual engrams.

An engram is severe in the exact ratio that it is conceived by the organism to have been a moment of threat to survival. The character of the threat and the perceptic content produces the aberration. A number of engrams with similar perceptics (*engram chain*) in an individual produce a complex aberration pattern which nevertheless has for its parts individual engrams.

Example: Engram received at the age of three and one-half years. Adult subject. As child in dental chair against his will, under antagonistic conditions, given nitrous oxide and tricked by dentist. During painful portion of treatment the dentist says, "He is asleep. He can't hear, feel or see anything. Stay there."

The perceptics which can be restimulated in this are the quality, pitch and volume of the dentist's voice; the sound of the dentist's drill; the slap of the cable running the drill; street noises of a specific kind;

the tactile of the mouth being forcibly held open; the smell of the mask; the sound of running water; the smell of nitrous oxide and, in short, several of each perceptic class, excluding only sight.

The effect of this experience, being a part of an engram chain which contained two earlier experiences (*precursors*), was in some small degree to trance the individual and maintain some portion of him in a regressed state.

This engram is too brief and extraordinarily simple, but it will serve as an example to the auditor. The timeless quality of the suggestions, the conceived antagonism, precursors on the engram chain awakened and reinforced—all these things confused the time sense with the individual and were otherwise reactive in later life.

An aberration is the manifestation of an engram and is serious only when it influences the competence of the individual in his environment.

Engrams are of two types, depending upon the duration of restimulation. There are *floaters* and *chronics*. A *floater* has not been restimulated during the lifetime succeeding it in the individual. A *chronic* is an engram which has been more or less continuously restimulated so that it has become an apparent portion of the individual. A chronic begins to gather locks. A floater has not accumulated locks, since it has never been restimulated.

A *lock* is a painful mental experience. It is or is not regarded by the analytical mind as a source of difficulty or aberration. It is a period of mental anguish and is wholly dependent upon an engram for its pain value. A lock can be conceived to be joined to an engram in such a way that it can be reached by the multiple scanners of the analytical mind which cannot reach the engram. When an engram is activated into a chronic, it accumulates numerous locks along the time track of the individual. The engram itself is not immediately locatable, except somatically, along the time track of the individual. Locks are of some diagnostic value, but as they exist as experiences more or less recallable by the analytical mind, they can be depended upon to vanish upon the removal of the engram from the reactive mind without further therapy.

The treating of a lock as a lock has some therapeutic value, but the exhaustion of locks from an aberrated individual is long and arduous and is seldom productive of any lasting result. Upon the location and exhaustion of the engram from the reactive mind, all of its locks vanish. An engram may exist unactivated as a floater for any number of years or for the entire duration of an individual's life. At any future moment after the receipt of an engram, whether that time period consists of days or decades, the floater may reactivate into a lock, at which time it becomes part of the commands obeyed by the analytical mind in its efforts to rationalize. The removal of the individual from his restimulators (which is to say, the environment in which the engram was reactive) is in itself a form of therapy, since the engram may then return to its status as a floater. But such a return will not remove the locks which the analytical mind can then recall as painful experiences.

Example: Engram: At birth occurs the phrase "No good" uttered during a moment of headache and gasping on the part of a child.

Lock: At the age of seven, the mother, in a fit of rage while the child was ill with a minor malady, said that he was "No good."

The removal of the engram also removes, ordinarily without further attention, the lock.

Note: Birth remained inactive in the above case as a floater until the moment of reduced analytical power at the age of seven when a birth phrase was repeated. It is worth remarking that the entire content of the birth engram is given simultaneously both to the child and to the mother, with only the difference of somatics. It is further worthy of note that the mother quite often perceives in the child a restimulator and uses against it the phrases which were said when the child gave the mother the greatest pain—namely, birth. The child is then victimized into various psychosomatic ills by the repetition of its birth engram restimulators, which ills may develop even more seriously into actual disease.

The mind controls the multiple and complex functions of the growth and condition of the organism. Containing organic sensation as one of its perceptics, the engram then, when reactivated, causes a somatic and additionally may deny body fluids (i.e., hormones and blood) to some portion of the anatomy, occasioning psychosomatic ills. The denial of fluid or adequate blood supply may result in a potentially infective area. The psychosomatic reduces the resistance of some portion of the body to actual disease.

Somatic and other sensory errors find their basis in unconscious antagonistic moments. A somatic may be adjusted by an address to a lock, but the permanency of adjustment obtains only until such time as the engram is again reactivated, causing another lock.

All aberrations are occasioned by engrams.

The physio-animal mind of an organism never ceases recording in some level. The exact moment when recording begins in an organism has not, at this date, been accurately determined. It has been found to be very early, probably earlier than four months after conception and five months before birth. In the presence of pain, any moment prior to the age of two years may be considered to be unanalytical. Any painful experience received by the fetus contains its full perceptic package, including darkness.

Once an auditor has worked a *prenatal engram* and has seen its influence upon the engram chain and the awake life of the adult, no question will remain in his mind concerning the actuality of the experience. That the fetus does record is attributable to a phenomenon of the extension of perceptions during moments of pain and the absence of the analytical mind.

Laboratory experiment demonstrates that under hypnosis an individual's sensory perception may be artificially extended.

The existence of pain in any large degree is sufficient to extend the hearing of the fetus so that it records, during the existence of pain and the presence of exterior sound, the entire and complete record of the experience. As a chronic engram is but precariously fixed on the mind, the syllables or voice timbres contained in the prenatal will reactivate the somatic and the emotional engramic content whenever the approximations of that engram appear in the child's (or the adult's) vicinity.

The understanding of language is not necessary to reactivate an engram, since the recording of the mind is so precise that the utterance of the identical words in similar tones during later prenatal periods, or during birth or immediately after birth, can and may occasion the original prenatal or any of the prenatals to become reactive—producing locks, injuring the health of the infant or, for that matter, of the fetus.

The perceptics of the fetus are extended only during moments of pain. But a chain of prenatal engrams can occasion a condition wherein the hearing of the fetus is chronically extended, forming numerous locks before birth. These locks will vanish when the actual engrams are discovered and exhausted from the psyche.

Any painful unanalytical moment containing antagonism is not only a matter of record, but a source of potential action in the human organism at any period during its lifetime—reserving, of course, the question of when the fetus first begins to record.

Birth is ordinarily a severely painful unconscious experience. It is ordinarily an engram of some magnitude. Anyone who has been born, then, possesses at least one engram.

Any period of absence of analytical power during receipt of physical pain has some engramic value.

Moments when the analytical power is present in some quantity, when physical pain is absent and only antagonism to the organism is present do not form engrams and are *not* responsible for the aberration of the individual.

Sociological maladjustments, parental punishments of a minor sort (even when they include pain), libidos, childhood struggles and jealousies are not capable of aberrating the individual. These can influence the personality and environment adjustment of the individual. But so long as he is not pathologically incompetent, he can and will resolve these problems and remain without aberration.

The human mind is an enormously powerful organism and its analytical ability is great. It is not overlaid above naturally unsocial or evil desires, but is founded upon powerful and constructive basics which only powerful, painful and antagonistic experiences can impede. Engrams will be found to have been conceived by the individual as intensely antagonistic to the survival of the organism.

The discovery of the *basic engram* is the first problem of the auditor. It normally results in an engram chain. The content of that chain will be found to be physically severe.

An engram is physically painful, is conceived by the organism as an antagonistic threat to its survival and is received during the absence of the analytical power of the mind. These factors may vary within the engram so that an engram may be of minimal pain, maximal antagonism and minimal absence of the analytical power, but no engram is available to the scanners of the consciousness.

ATTENTION: ONE HAS AS MUCH FUNCTIONING ANALYZER AS ONE HAS AWARENESS OF "NOW."

The body is to some degree re-undergoing the experience of the engram whenever the experience is restimulated. A chronic psychosomatic, such as a painful arm, indicates the chronic, continuous co-existence with "now" of the moment the arm is broken or hurt. Several engrams reactivated into a chronic state bring several moments of unconsciousness, pain and antagonism into a co-existence with "now." The engram is a bundle of perceptics which include, as the primary manifestation, organic sensation. The organic sensation is enforced on the members of the body to a greater or lesser degree whenever and as long as the engram is restimulated. There is only *one* psychosomatic which is common to all engrams. Any engram contains this as part of the command it will enforce upon the body. The analytical mind is an organism and a part of the human body. As a stomach may be made to ache chronically (ulcers), to feel "broken" the engram also enforces a command upon the *organ* of the analytical mind. That command is common to every engram. Engrams are valid only when they are received during a momentary dispersal of shocked null condition of the analytical mind.

EVERY ENGRAM CONTAINS AND ENFORCES THE COMMAND ON THE ANALYTICAL MIND THAT *IT HAS BEEN DISPERSED AND IS NOT OPERATING.*

This is common to every engram. This is reduction of the intellect by engrams, totally aside from specific engramic content. It explains at once insanity and the remarkable mental facility of a Clear.

Chapter Six

ABERRATIONS

Aberrations

A ll *aberrations* of any kind are of precisely the same nature (as covered in the last chapter). It is the content of the engram which causes the aberration and forms its nature. Complexity among engramic contents may demonstrate a most complex aberration.

The various commands contained in the engrams, reactivating and modifying the basic dynamic command of the mind, produce abnormal characteristics in the behavior of the analytical mind which are chronic or sporadic as the engrams occasioning them are restimulated. An entire concept of existence may be built from engramic content. Conflicts in the commands contained in engrams and conflicts between the basic dynamic and the engramic content combine into behavior patterns.

When the organism has become so aberrated that it can no longer adapt itself to this environment, it can be considered to be insane in that environment. Change of environment may relieve the condition or, more certainly, the exhaustion of the content of the reactive mind will restore the ability of the analytical mind to solve the problems with which it is confronted.

Whatever the engramic content of the reactive mind and its potential influence upon the behavior of the individual, it does not necessarily follow that the reactive mind may be chronically restimulated. However, when the reactive mind has been restimulated consistently, the analytical mind called upon to solve the problems around and through antagonistic and incorrect data may be unable to perform its task. In the absence of disease or injury, any mind not in a physiological amentia state may be restored to normal function by the removal of the reactive mind. It should be noted, however, that this is modified by the fact that individuals who have received insulin shocks, prefrontal lobotomies, electric shocks and other shock treatments are regarded as equivocal and are temporarily classed with disease cases for lack of adequate observation in this stage of the experimental research.

People can be regarded as rational or irrational only insofar as they react in their customary environment. But any individual in possession of a reactive mind is an unknown quantity until that reactive mind has been examined. If he has been examined, his mind can be cleared in the same process.

There are several factors which may be contained in the engrams in the reactive mind which most certainly tend toward aberration. These include engramic commands which derange the time sense of the individual and thus apparently destroy his time track—engrams which contain restimulators of such timelessness and such perceptic content that they remain thereafter continually with the individual and seem to arrest him or regress him in time.

Engrams which contain commands that make the individual chronically unable to conceive differences are especially harmful, since these tend to compare everything to engramic value and thus cause the individual to arrive at a chronic state of engramic thinking.

The mind is an organism which resolves problems related to survival, utilizing its ability to conceive similarities and observe differences.

Engrams which destroy or tend to hold in suspension the analytical mind's ability to conceive associations most influence the apparent intelligence of the mind. But engrams which tend, by their command content, to destroy the mind's ability to conceive differences may produce severe aberration.

"*Engrams which contain commands that make the individual chronically unable to conceive differences are especially harmful, since these tend to compare everything to engramic value and thus cause the individual to arrive at a chronic state of engramic thinking.*"

Example: "All men are alike," received as powerful engramic content, would tend to compare every man and associate him with those men contained in the reactive mind as painful and dangerous.

An aberration may attain any form or complexion. As a rough analogy, a *compulsion* may be conceived to be an engramic command that the organism *must* do something; a *repression* is a command that the organism must *not* do something; a *neurosis* is an emotional state containing conflicts and emotional data inhibiting the abilities or welfare of the individual; and a *psychosis* is a conflict of commands which seriously reduce the individual's ability to solve his problems in his environment to a point where he cannot adjust himself to some vital phase of his environmental needs.

All this variety of manifestation of aberration is occasioned by the pain-enforced commands or contents of engrams.

Physical aberrations are occasioned by engrams when they are not the result of injury or disease. Even then the aspect may be improved by the exhaustion of the reactive mind of the sick individual. The engram cannot manifest itself as a mental aberration without also manifesting itself to some degree as somatic aberration. Removal of the somatic content of engrams, which is also necessary to obtain any other relief, can and does occasion glandular readjustment, cellular growth, cellular inhibition and other physiological corrections.

Chapter Seven

THE TONE SCALE

The Tone Scale

The *Tone Scale* denotes numerically, first, the status of an engram in the reactive mind, next, its progress during work, and provides a measure of sanity in an individual.

The derivation of this scale is clinical and is based upon observation of engrams during work. When an engram is located and developed, the extreme range it can follow begins with *apathy,* develops into *anger* (or the various facets of antagonism), proceeds into *boredom* and arrives at last in *cheerfulness* or vanishes utterly.

The Tone Scale is essentially an assignation of numerical value by which engrams and individuals can be numerically classified. It is not arbitrary, but will be found to approximate some actual governing law in nature.

Tone 0 is equivalent to death. An engram with 0 tone would be a death engram. An individual with a 0 tone would be dead.

Ranging upward from 0 to 1 is then that emotional bracket which may be denoted as apathy, along its graduated scale from death to the beginnings of apathetic resentment.

From 1 to 2 is the range of antagonism, including suspicion, resentment and anger.

Boredom and its equivalents, by which is denoted minor annoyance, begins at 2 and ends at 3.

From 3 to 4 are the emotions which range from carelessness to cheerfulness.

The term *Tone 4* denotes an engram or an individual who has achieved complete rationality and cheerfulness.

The decimal scale can be used from 0.0 to 4.0 to approximate the emotional value of engrams and their ability to impede the dynamics.

Each engram residual in the reactive mind has its own independent tonal value. Serious engrams will be found in the apathy range. Dangerous engrams will be found in the anger range. Above 2.5 an engram could not be considered to have any great value in affecting the analytical mind. Each engram in the reactive mind, then, can be said to possess a tone value. The composite sum of these engrams will give, if added, a numerical value to the reactive mind.

Engrams can be computed as they lie along the dynamics and to each dynamic may be assigned a tone. The sum of the tones of the dynamics divided by the number of the dynamics will give a potential numerical value for an individual. This, of course, is variable, depending on the existence of restimulators in his environment to reactivate the engrams. The general tone of an individual is important both in diagnosis and in establishing a resolution to the case.

The probable average of Mankind, at this writing, may be in the vicinity of 3.0. Complete rationality depends upon exhaustion of the reactive mind and complete rationality is invariably the result of reaching Tone 4.

The initial diagnosis for a person in Dianetics is done by the assignation of a general tone to denote the condition of his reactive mind. His methods of meeting life, his emotional reaction to the problems in his environment can be evaluated by the use of the Tone Scale.

In therapy, as will be covered later, an engram normally can be expected to run from its initial value in the apathy or anger range to Tone 4. Very shortly after it reaches Tone 4, it should vanish. If it vanishes without attaining the laughter of Tone 4, it can be assumed that the individual's basic engram has not been erased.

The Tone Scale has value in the therapy and should be thoroughly understood.

The Tone Scale

Chapter Eight

The Character of Engrams

The Character of Engrams

There are several general *types of engrams*. It must be understood that the mind possesses a *time track* of one sort or another and that this track is a specific thing. The time track of an individual will include all those things available to his analytical mind, but the data which he can easily contact along his time track is definitely not engramic even if it possesses an emotional charge. Everything on this track will be rational or justified experience. It will not include engrams. It may include locks or even *engram locks*—which is to say that it may include moments of mental anguish or antagonism and may even include instants of unconsciousness which have some slight engramic value and which are locks on some engram.

An engram has several specific, positive characteristics. It is received by the individual at some moment of physical pain. It is not available to the analyzer. And it includes conceived or actual antagonism to the survival of the organism. Certain mechanisms, such as "Forget it," may swerve a minimally painful or unconscious experience off the time track. In that case, it becomes possessed of engramic value.

All engrams with power to derange the analytical mind and aberrate the physical body lie off the time track and are not available to the analytical mind without auditor assistance.

By reason of its disorganization during the moment the engram was received, or because it has been forcibly instructed that the data in the engram is not to be recalled, the analyzer cannot reach the engram by ordinary means because the data has been erroneously labeled "Dangerous," "Important" or "Too painful to touch." The engram then, by a bypass circuit, feeds hidden commands into the analyzer. By a direct instantaneous circuit, it is permanently connected to the motor controls, all perceptic channels, the glands and heart. It is awaiting a moment of low general tone, weariness or injury when the analytical mind has reduced powers. It is also awaiting the perception of one or more of the engram's restimulators in the environment of the organism.

Continuous restimulation of the engrams can in itself cause a low general tone, which in its turn permits more engrams to become restimulated. As the reactive mind comes into a more or less completely chronic state of reaction, the individual becomes more and more governed by this mind. His thought becomes more and more engramic and he can be seen to drop in general tone on the Tone Scale down to the break point, which may be arbitrarily placed somewhere between 2.0 and 2.5 and below which lies the region of insanity.

Engramic thought is irrational identity-thought, by which the mind is made to conceive identities where only vague similarities may exist. It is necessary that the auditor thoroughly understand engramic thought, for it is with this complete irrationality of identity that he will basically deal. As he works with any individual, sane or insane, he must continually employ in the bulk of his computation on the case the equation of engramic thinking.

Engramic thinking can be stated by: $A=A=A=A=A$.

The engram, when one or more of its restimulators is perceived in the environment during a moment of low general tone, may dramatize. The dramatization *is* the precise content of the engram. The aberration *is* the precise content of the engram. The reaction of an individual's analytical mind when an engram is reactivated *is* justification.

There is reason to believe that part of this survival mechanism consists of the axiom:

THE ANALYZER MUST NEVER PERMIT AN INCORRECT SOLUTION.

The engram brings about many incorrect solutions. The analyzer may very well become entirely involved with the attempt to discover and deliver to a society, or to itself, adequate rational reasons for the behavior of the organism.

The analytical mind, though working from the command of the engram itself, is unaware of the source of the command. Not being able to discover the source, it introverts more and more in an effort to solve a problem which contains danger to the organism. The analytical mind tends to find the danger without and within the organism.

There are five ways that the organism can react to a danger in its vicinity. It can *attack* it, *avoid* it, *neglect* it, *run* from it or *succumb* to it. In just these ways can the analytical mind, which it must be remembered *is* possessed of self-determinism and willpower, react to the reactive mind. As the general tone lowers, which is to say, as the analytical mind becomes less and less powerful through weariness, continual reverses in general health, etc., the more and more heed it must give to the problems unsolved in the reactive mind. These are in essence unsolved problems. As such, they contain their own solutions. The analytical mind, unable to reach them, justifies the organism's reaction to them (succumbs to them), causes the organism to attempt to flee from them, apathetically may neglect them (as in prefrontal lobotomy), avoids them in many intricate ways or attacks them. The analytical mind is not only not certain where the experience lies on the time track, it also does not know whether the menace is within the organism or without it. So, it can become entirely indiscriminate and eventually it may achieve highly irrational solutions by which it seeks to solve the problems of the highly irrational reactive mind.

The deep sensory perception channel entering the mind is evidently equipped with an *appreciator* which sorts according to the momentary general tone or potential of the analytical mind. The higher the general tone or potential of the analytical mind, the better the data in the appreciator is sorted. The appreciator circuits are evidently fully apprised of engramic content in the reactive mind and evaluate restimulators perceived in the environment against the general tone of the analytical mind. When that is low, restimulators route more or less directly to the reactive mind which instantly responds by fixed connections into the motor controls. Commands to the various members, muscles, glands and organs of the body may be sporadic or constant, producing a high variety of responses in the body. Entire vocabularies are fed into the voice circuits directly from the reactive mind when an engram is restimulated. Orders to be active or inactive are fed to other portions. The individual time track of the engram spaces the commands to the organism and a dramatization is accomplished which may contain a portion or all of the content of the engram, as governed by the situation. Psychosomatic ills, hysterias, rages, tantrums, criminal acts and any and all content prejudicial to the survival of the organism in which the organism is seen to be indulging, has as its source the reactive mind.

The sole and only content of the reactive mind is *what exterior sources have done to the organism.*

None of the content of the reactive mind is self-motivated. The auditor is then interested only in what is done *to* the person, not what the person himself has done, since for purposes of therapy the acts of the organism in its society can be discounted beyond diagnosis. Even then, they are of small importance to the auditor.

An organism possessed of an analytical mind not victimized by incapacitating disease or injury and unaberrated will commit no act knowingly prejudicial to the survival of the organism or other factors within the dynamics. It will combat only those dangers in society which are actual menaces.

Whatever may be the status of the "innate moral sense," the basic intent of the basic personality is to further various energy forms along the dynamic toward the goal. Only moments of actual dispersal of the awareness of the analytical mind permit data to be received which is prejudicial to the intent of the dynamics. Only from these unconscious moments can the basically stable and enormously powerful and able analytical mind be aberrated through the implantation of unanalyzed, painfully administered and antagonistic information. It is the purpose of the auditor to find and exhaust these moments from the life of the individual. This therapy includes, therefore, as its basic principle, the exhaustion of all the painfully unconscious moments of a person's life. By eradicating pain from the life of an individual, the auditor returns the individual to complete rationality and sanity.

The auditor should never be content with merely bringing the individual back to normal. He should achieve with the individual a Tone 4 even though this is far in advance of the average state of society at this time. A Tone 4 with his dynamics intact and powerful, with his rationality and intelligence increased to the optimum, becomes extremely valuable to the society, whatever his past.

Knowing this, the auditor can expect a maximum result of lasting duration with any person not physically hopeless.

An auditor in Dianetics will achieve the best results by ignoring impulses to educate or inform the individual in any way beyond instructions sufficient to acquire cooperation.

The entire purpose of the auditor is to rehabilitate the basic dynamic, the four dynamics and the normal purpose or profession of the individual. Anything implanted by positive suggestion or education in the course of therapy is harmful and must be cancelled if delivered. Only the basic personality of the individual can decide and evaluate things in his environment. Therefore, hypnotism as practiced with positive suggestion is shunned, since any and all hypnotic commands with the attendant forgetter mechanisms are no more than artificially implanted engrams. Indeed, it is quite usual for the auditor to have to exhaust hypnotically implanted material received either from some hypnotist or from the individual's analytical mind itself when he is operating under "self-control." Hypnotism, as such, does not work and a study and short practice in Dianetics will reveal exactly why.

The auditor is attempting to delete the reactive mind from the individual. This reactive mind is an infestation of foreign, careless and unreasoning commands which disrupt the self-determinism of the individual to such an extent that he no longer has charge, through his analytical mind, of the organism itself, but finds himself under the continual and chronic orders of unseen, never-reviewed exterior forces, often and usually antipathetic to the survival of the organism.

Engrams deal with identities where no identities exist. They therefore pose many strange and irrational problems which are seen as aberrations in people. If a human being has been born and not cleared, he can be supposed to have at least one engram. Anyone who has a birth which has not been cleared by therapy has, therefore, a reactive mind. There is no disgrace attached to having a reactive mind, since it was thrust, without his consent and without his knowledge, upon an unconscious and helpless individual. Sometimes this was done by people with the best of imaginable intentions. A person not possessed of a rational mind cannot be rationally considered to be morally responsible no matter the demands of the current society, which hitherto lacked any method of determining responsibility.

The pain contained in the reactive mind is normally severe. The usual parental punishments, family complications, reprimands, minor accidents and the battle of the individual with his environment influence, but do not cause, a reactive mind. Nor do these things have the power to change materially the reactions of an individual.

In the background of any individual exist many hidden personalities contained in the reactive mind. Dealing in identities, the reactive mind often confuses identities of individuals. Therefore, irrational attachments and antipathies are formed by aberrated individuals who can often find no reason for such attachments or antipathies in their contemporary environment.

*"If a human being has been born and not cleared,
he can be supposed to have at least one engram.
Anyone who has a birth which has not been cleared
by therapy has, therefore, a reactive mind."*

The content of an engram is literally interpreted, not as it was stated to the unconscious individual, but as it was received in its most literal phraseology and perception.

The organism possesses many inherent mechanisms and abilities by which it can learn or preserve or forward itself along the dynamic. Any one of them may be exaggerated by engrams to a point where it becomes an actual threat to the organism or aberrates it. Engrams can and do aberrate all the sensory perceptions, any and all parts of the body and the mind itself. By demanding suicide, the engram can destroy the entire organism.

The error of the reactive mind was introduced by the evolution of speech, for which the basic mechanism was not designed. When all perceptics, save speech, formed the reactive mind, it was to some degree serviceable. With speech came such complexities of perception and such interchanges of ideas that a whole series of illusions and delusions could be derived from the reactive mind's necessity to determine identities for purposes of emergency.

Without the reactive type mind, survival would be extremely difficult, since it must be there to care for emergencies during moments of dispersal of the analytical mind by shock or other means.

With speech, the reactive mind came to possess far more power and extensive content. The analytical mind, being a delicate mechanism in some respects, no matter how rugged and capable in others, then could become subjected to delusions and illusions which, however shadowy and unreal, must nevertheless be obeyed. By stripping the reactive mind of its past painful content, the analytical mind may be placed in complete command of the organism.

The moment a man or a group becomes possessed of this ability, it becomes possessed of self-determinism. So long as these possess reactive minds, irrationalities will persist. Because it contains literal speech, no reactive mind can be conceived to be of any value whatsoever to the rational organism. Since the methods of that reactive mind remain intact and will continue to act to preserve the organism in times of unconsciousness of the analytical mind, there is no residual good in any reactive mind. It is capable of any illusion.

It has no assist power along the dynamics, save only to cancel or modify other reactive mind content. The source of the individual's power and purpose is not derived from the reactive mind, but from the basic dynamic and from the four dynamics. Any auditor will establish this to his own satisfaction after he has cleared a very few cases.

When an individual is attempting to "hold on to his aberrations," the auditor may be assured that that person has, as part of the content of the reactive mind, such phrases as "Don't dare get rid of it" which, identically translated, apparently applies to aberrations. It may, in fact, apply in an engram containing an attempted abortion.

The identity factor in the reactive mind may cause the analytical mind to respond irrationally to treatment and to justify the aberrations in many irrational ways. Whatever means he uses or statements he makes to avoid the exhaustion of his reactive mind is contained exactly in the reactive mind as a positive suggestion and has no application whatsoever in rational thought.

Individuality, if by that is meant a man's desires and habits, is not traced to the reactive mind, save when by "individuality" is meant those flagrant eccentricities which pass in Dickens for characters.

A man is much more individual after his reactive mind has been cleared.

Part II

Auditing

DIANETICS: THE ORIGINAL THESIS

Chapter Nine

The Auditor's Code

The Auditor's Code

Not because it is a pleasant thing to do or because it is a noble idea, the auditor must always treat a *preclear** in a certain definite way which can be outlined as the *Auditor's Code.* Failure to follow this code will cause trouble to the auditor, will considerably lengthen and disturb his work and may endanger the preclear.

The auditor, in the first place, at the optimum should be himself a Clear. Otherwise he will find that many of his own engrams are restimulated as he listens to the engrams of his preclears. This restimulation may cause his own engrams to become chronic, victimizing him with various allergies and delusions and causing him to be, at best, extremely uncomfortable.

An auditor can audit while he himself is being cleared as this is a peculiar and special method of locating his own engrams, since they become restimulated. Becoming painful to him, they can be found and speedily removed.

Even if he is not himself cleared, the auditor must act like a Clear toward the preclear. The Auditor's Code is the natural activity of a Clear.

The auditor must act toward the preclear exactly in the way that the preclear, as an organism, would desire that his own conscious analytical mind would react to and consider the organism.

---

*Preclear: an individual entered upon Dianetic therapy (auditing) for the purpose of being cleared.

"The auditor must act toward the preclear
exactly in the way that the preclear,
as an organism, would desire that his
own conscious analytical mind would
react to and consider the organism."

An affinity must therefore be maintained at all costs. The auditor must never permit himself to lose his temper, become aggravated, to scold or badger or antagonize the preclear in any way. To do so would not merely disturb the comfort of the preclear, but might additionally derange him and might even prohibit further beneficial auditing by that auditor.

The code is nearly "Christlike."

The auditor must be *confident,* in that he must continually reassure the preclear when restimulated engrams cause despondency on the preclear's part. A cheerful, optimistic presence encourages the preclear through his most painful experiences.

The auditor must be *courageous,* never permitting himself to be intimidated by either the aggression or hostility of the preclear.

The auditor must be *kind,* never indulging in hostilities or personal prejudices.

The auditor must be *trustworthy,* never betraying or capriciously denying a preclear and, above all, never breaking his word to the preclear.

An auditor must be *clean,* for personal odors or bad breath may be restimulators to the preclear or may disturb him.

The auditor must take care *not to offend* the concepts or sensibilities of the preclear.

The auditor must be *persistent,* never permitting the case of the preclear to either resist him or to remain unsolved until it is in a proper Tone 4, since the restimulation of engrams is a malady unto itself unless they are being properly exhausted.

The auditor must be *patient,* never hurrying or harassing the preclear beyond the needs of stirring an engram into view. He must be willing to work at any and all times necessary, for the length of time necessary to exhaust the engram in process of elimination.

In addition to these things, it may be remarked that a definite affinity is established between the auditor and preclear during the time of auditing. In the case of opposite sexes, this affinity may amount to an infatuation. The auditor must remain aware of this and know that he can and should redirect the infatuation to some person or activity other than himself when auditing is at end. Not to do so is to produce an eventual situation wherein the preclear may have to be rebuffed, with consequent trouble for the auditor at the end of therapy.

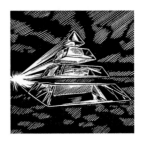

Chapter Ten

AUDITING

Auditing

T he *auditing* technique consists of assisting the preclear's analytical mind with the auditor's analytical mind. The auditor then functions during each successive period of auditing, and only during the periods of auditing, as an additional analytical mind of the preclear.

The reactive mind was received during the dispersal or inactivity of the analytical mind. The reactive mind is removed by *returning* the preclear to the engram and laying its contents before the scrutiny of the analytical mind.

The technique of auditing is done in what is called a Dianetic *reverie*. The preclear sits in a comfortable chair with arms, or lies on a couch in a quiet room where perceptic distractions are minimal. The auditor tells him to look at the ceiling. The auditor says, "When I count from one to seven your eyes will close." The auditor then counts from one to seven and keeps counting quietly and pleasantly until the preclear closes his eyes.

This is the entire routine. Consider it more a signal that proceedings are to begin and a means of concentrating the preclear on his own concerns and the auditor than anything else. *This is not hypnotism.* It is vastly different. The preclear knows everything which is going on around him. He is not "asleep" and he can bring himself out of it anytime he likes.

The auditor makes very sure that the preclear is not hypnotized by telling him, before he begins to count, "You will know everything which goes on. You will be able to remember everything that happens. You can exercise your own control. If you do not like what is happening, you can instantly pull out of it. Now, one, two, three, four," etc.

In reverie, the next words of the auditor should be devoted to the installing of a *canceller*. This should be worded in such a way that it will furnish a key word which, when spoken at the end of therapy, will cancel every slightest remark or suggestion made by the auditor while the preclear was in reverie. This is a guarantee that no positive suggestions will be left residual in the mind of the preclear through the inadvertent or accidental slips attendant to auditing. Such a canceller should also cancel the reverie, being worded with sufficient generality to take in anything and everything the auditor may say to the preclear during the entire period of therapy.

At no time should the auditor permit the preclear to be under the delusion that he is being treated by hypnosis. This is mentioned because hypnotism is a current fad and the principles of Dianetics have nothing whatever to do with hypnotism. Both are based upon simple natural laws, but have between them an enormous gulf. One is the tool of the charlatan and the other is the science of the human mind.

Returning is employed in Dianetic therapy. Returning is the method of retaining the body and the awareness of the preclear in present time while he is told to go back to a certain incident. Dates are not mentioned. His size is not mentioned. Various means are used to restimulate his memory. Any of the perceptics may be employed to return him to some period of his past. He is told simply to "Go back to the time when _____." He is returned and made to recount what he can of the incident. He is told he is "right there" and that he "can recall this." Little else is said by the auditor, save those hints necessary to return the preclear to the proper time. Wide awake, he can return to moments in the past.

"Returning is the method of retaining the body
and the awareness of the preclear in present time
while he is told to go back to a certain incident."

The preclear is not allowed at any moment to revivify in that period, since the data is drained as a surcharge from his time track to present time. He is told that he "can remember this," but he is never told that he "can remember this in present time" since that will occasion the somatics to return to present time. Most of the data is located by observing some somatic pain in the individual or some somatic aberration and seeking to discover wherein it was received.

The somatics are employed primarily because the *motor controls* possess a less disturbed time track than the *sensory strip*. It must be remembered that there is no aberration without an accompanying somatic. The somatics alone, being physical ills of one sort or another, hold the aberrated content of the reactive mind in place. The motor controls can be returned to a period although the conscious or analytical mind believes itself to be entirely in present time. By talking to the muscles or motor controls or various bodily aches and pains, the auditor can shift them at will up and down their time track. This time track is not connected to the analytical mind and speech, but is apparently a parallel time track with greater reliability than the sensory track. The precision of data contained in the motor control time track is enormous. Muscles can be made to tense or relax. Coughs, aches and pains can be made to come and go simply by uttering the right words for the engram, or the wrong words.

It is the primary task of the auditor to cause the time tracks of the motor strip and the sensory strip to come into parallel. That the time track exists in the strips has not been proven, but they can so be considered for the purposes of this explanation. That they exist is extremely apparent. The motor strip time track can be asked questions down to the smallest moment of time and the area of an engram can at times be so located. Its character can also be determined.

The lie detector, the encephalograph and many other means are useful in determining both the character and the extent of the engrams, since into these can be fed the restimulators of the preclear. A codified restimulator list can be created which will be found to be common to most preclears. It should include all types of illnesses, accidents, the common trite phrases of the society and names of various persons who commonly surround a child during his childhood. Such a codified restimulator list would be extremely valuable in therapy and every auditor can compose his own. These are best composed after the auditing of the individual preclear and after inquiry into his life to determine the various irrationalities of thought.

In that engrams are identity-thought, the remarks of the preclear about his engrams will be found to be included in the content of those engrams. When the preclear is asked to imagine a bad situation at certain ages and under hypothetical conditions, he will very often deliver up a complete engram. The auditor must realize that every remark that a preclear makes while he is being made to go over his reactive mind is probably some part of the content of that reactive mind. That mind is literal. The words the preclear uses when referring to it must be literally evaluated.

Chapter Eleven
DIAGNOSIS

Diagnosis

It is a useful and positive principle that whatever confronts or contests the analytical mind of the preclear will also confront and contest the analytical mind of the auditor. When the auditor is acting as an additional analytical mind of the preclear, whatever emotion or antagonism is directed toward him is the emotion or antagonism which is directed by the reactive mind toward the preclear's own analytical mind. If a preclear cannot hear what people are saying in his engrams, he has another engram about "Can't hear." If he cannot feel anything in his engram, it is because he has an engram about "Can't feel." If he cannot see, he has an engram about "Not being able to see," and so forth. If he cannot return, he has an engram about going back or returning to childhood or some such thing. If he is doubtful and skeptical about what is happening or what has happened to him, it is because he has an engram about being doubtful and skeptical. If he is antagonistic, his reactive mind contains a great deal of antagonism. If he is self-conscious or embarrassed, it is because his reactive mind contains self-consciousness or embarrassment. If he insists on maintaining his own control, refusing to do what the auditor tells him to do, it is because he has an engram about self-control. And so forth and so on. This is identity-thought. All this is used in *diagnosis*.

Auditing is the best method of learning the problems of the preclear. Trying to work the preclear into returning—hearing, seeing, feeling, going back and forward—and taking due note of what he says about the entire process will form a rather complete diagnosis on one who is not insane. Questioning the preclear as to what is wrong with him will elicit replies straight out of his principal engrams. Listening to an endless justification of his actions is both a delay and a waste of time, but listening to what he has to say about what he thinks has happened to him or what he is afraid of is of definite value.

Insane persons form and pose a slightly different, but essentially the same problem.

It is a clinically established observation that the reactive mind is relatively shallow. Below it lies the basic personality of the individual, no matter how "insane" he may be. Therefore, by one means or another, a rational being may be reached within a preclear, a being who is not aberrated. Here it can be established what the preclear really wants, what he hopes, what he actually feels. It has been observed that no matter what his raving state, providing his brain structure is normal and complete, the basic personality is entirely sound and sane and will cooperate. After auditing, the preclear will become this strong, competent and able personality.

The reactive mind, when unable to exert itself to its aberrated full in the environment of the preclear, will "break" the preclear, or cause him to lose tone. Therefore, it is of definite interest to discover what immediately preceded the break of the preclear or what is currently causing him unhappiness. Something is dispersing his dynamics. The probability is that he has a chronic restimulator in his vicinity. Wives, husbands, mothers, fathers, superiors, etc., can be the source of such breaking, since they turn the purpose of the reactive mind (which pretends to desire above all else the best interest of the preclear) back upon the preclear himself. Thus, these sources cause the preclear to lower back into the tone of the reactive mind (apathy or a low Tone 2).

The problem of the *fixed person* and the problem of the *sympathy engram* are both visible in the aberrated individual.

The identity-thought of the reactive mind has taken some part of the person of some individual in the preclear's current environment and referred it to some part of the person of an individual in the preclear's engramic past. The discovery of this identity is one of the principal problems of therapy. The sympathy engram is of a very specific nature, being the effort of the parent or guardian to be kind to a child who is severely hurt. If that parent or guardian has shown the child antagonism prior to the time of the injury, the adult (preclear) is prone to reactivate the injury in the presence of the identity personality with whom he is now associated. This causes many somatic ills to present themselves in the present. Only the exact words of a sympathy engram will soothe the aberrated personality.

There are not many personality types. A human being learns through mimicry. If his own self is found to be too painful, he can become another self and very often does. A Tone 4 can become people at will without being aberrated about it, thus enjoying books and plays by "being" the person portrayed. But an aberrated individual can become part of the engramic cast of his reactive mind and so solve all of his problems in such an aberrated fashion. Aberrated people are not themselves, since they do not possess their own determinism.

As has been stated, those emotions, doubts, worries and problems, which confront the auditor when attempting to work the preclear while returned, will lead the auditor into the basic content of the reactive mind.

There are certain definite manifestations which can be suspected and certain routines which follow every case. Every human being has been carried in the womb and every human being has been born. The discovery of the *basic engram* is extremely necessary for the commencement of auditing. Finding the basic engram is like taking the enemy in the flank. There is nothing before it. Therefore, the end most remote from the adult life of the individual is the end most exposed for the attack of the auditor.

In the basic engram, the preclear can see, feel, hear and freely emote. When he is returned to later incidents, it may be found that he cannot do these things, no matter how hard the auditor works to enable him to do so. By pursuing the engram chain up its chronological sequence, this ability will be restored. Therefore, it is necessary, first and foremost, to locate the basic engram. This may, in some few cases, lie later than birth. In the majority of the cases, it will be found to lie at or before birth. No discussion is here entered about the ability of the human mind to remember at such remote periods. It can be stated, however, that when engramic data does exist, the time track is opened by pain and antagonism at these extreme points and can be contacted and exhausted. The analytical mind is not present at these moments. Quite in addition to this, the engrams are not even on the open time track. It is with the greatest difficulty that the auditor will find the basic engram. Since it is ordinarily quite painful and the scanning mechanism has as its purpose (or one of its purposes) the avoidance of pain, it will not easily reach them. Like the scanning mechanism on a cathode ray tube, the scanners of the analytical mind sweep over, skipping and not touching, the data on the engram chain. By various means, the auditor must then force the preclear's scanners to contact that data and force the data back onto the time track where it can be properly exhausted.

Light prenatals are the best possible approach to a case. When the only prenatal is an extremely heavy one or an attempted abortion (which, by the way, are very common), the auditor must use a great deal of guile. It can be said that the basic engram and the beginning of the actual engram chain is early (before, near or during birth), is painful and will not be easily contacted. In that few preclears have more than a score of serious engrams, the task is light when once begun, but requires a great deal of imagination and persuasion.

A prenatal must always be suspected unless birth, when lifted, rises easily into a Tone 4. If none of the engrams will rise into a Tone 4, the auditor would suppose that he has not discovered the basic. There are three kinds of engrams: the *precursor,* the *engram* and the *follower.* By "engram" here is meant that experience which the auditor has found and is working upon. If it does not seem to be lifting after a few recountings, a precursor must be suspected and returned to. In this way, an earlier basic may be discovered. But it is a fruitless task and wasted energy to attempt to work anything but a basic. Blows in the womb, attempted abortions and birth are the usual basics. These must be exhausted to their fullest degree before other engrams are even glanced at. The advantage of this is that everyone has a birth. Birth can be looked for. If it is not quickly found and if it does not develop on examination, then an earlier experience must be suspected and located if possible. In this way, the prenatals may be discovered. Easily, the most important are the prenatals.

When a child is abnormally afraid of the dark, he probably has a prenatal experience. This prenatal experience will include all the sound data and sensory data of the incident. It is eidetic and identical. The preclear will have somatics. These, on the first few recountings, will be ordinarily faint and then become more severe as more data is located. The data will finally be in more or less a complete state and the engram will begin to lift, rising up through the various tones. All prenatals are apathy experiences and are therefore serious.

Minor taps and discomforts in the womb are of no consequence. A true engram will consist of such a thing as a knitting needle being rammed through the fetus, half of the fetus' head being badly injured, blows of various kinds bringing about fetal unconsciousness and so forth. Returning will find an opening into any period when there has been pain.

Disbeliefs and antagonisms from the preclear on the subject of such a thing as an attempted abortion should be overlooked by the auditor or taken into account as the sign of an existing engram. A case is recalled wherein a girl insisted that if an abortion had ever been attempted on her, it should have been successful. Through several sessions, while an attempt was made to lift birth, she continued this assertion until the auditor realized that this was probably a remark made by the abortionist (or the mother) when his efforts failed. As soon as this was suggested to the girl, she was able to at last reach the incident with its somatics without any further suggestion from the auditor. A chronic apathy case under treatment for some years in an institution, she suddenly responded to treatment, brought the abortion to Tone 4, erased birth to Tone 4 and recovered mentally and physically into a social asset well above normal.

The auditor should continue to suspect prenatals so long as he cannot get later engrams easily into Tone 4. Once an engram chain has been lifted at its end nearest to conception, the preclear should begin to clear relatively automatically, aided but little by the auditor. The clear should be in terms of laughter, at its optimum. This laughter is the reversing of charges, residual in the locks and engram locks, which depended for their fear content or antagonistic content upon the basic engrams.

Little engramic data of any importance is to be found after the age of ten, although a serious operation or accident might provide one. The bulk of the engram data will be found before the age of two. The most important data is ordinarily in the period of infancy, birth or prenatal, with the latter containing the preponderance of the important data.

Abortion attempts are easy to recognize when an auditor has had some experience. The parent who attempted the abortion will, after birth, likely be a source of anxiety to the individual, who seems to require a great deal of affection and attention from that parent. The individual will be found to be most fond of the parent (or other) who did not aid or who actually tried to prevent the abortion attempt. At this time abortion attempts are extremely common.

When an abortion attempt has been lifted, the engram chain should easily be brought to the time track and exhausted by the auditor.

Auditing is essentially very simple, but it demands precise understanding of the principles involved and imagination and sympathy on the part of the auditor. He must learn to compute engramically, or learn to think with his analytical mind (only for the purposes of therapy to others) engramically. His biggest problem is the discovery of the actual basic. It may elude him for a considerable period of time.

"The bulk of the engram data will be found
before the age of two. The most important data is
ordinarily in the period of infancy, birth or prenatal,
with the latter containing the preponderance
of the important data."

There is other preparatory work to do in a case than the discovery of the basic. Occasionally an entire time track must be rehabilitated in cases in which "Do not remember" and "Can't remember" have obscured the track. A few later locks can be found and exhausted in the same manner that engrams are exhausted and the track can be restored. The hysteria or fear of the individual can be momentarily allayed one way or the other and the problem of reaching the basic can be entered upon. There are as many types of cases as there are cases, but these are the primary fundamentals.

An auditor must think his way through every case, taking as his data the constantly reiterated statements of the preclear during auditing and accumulating experience as to how incidents can be thrust off the time track, burying them from sight of the analytical mind, thus forming a reactive mind to the detriment of the organism.

Chapter Twelve
Exhaustion of Engrams

Exhaustion of Engrams

The technique of *exhausting an engram* is not complicated, but it must be adhered to. An engram is an unconscious moment containing physical pain and conceived or actual antagonism to the organism. Therefore, that engram, before it is discovered, will exhibit antagonism toward the auditor trying to discover it. When it is first discovered, it may be found to be lacking in its essential data. There are many techniques by which this data can be developed. In a prenatal engram, the analytical mind apparently must redevelop the situation. Many returns to the incident are therefore necessary. The preclear is returned to the incident and is told that the next time he is returned to this place, he will remember everything about the incident. He is then taken up to present time and addressed on some other subject. Immediately after, he is returned to the supposed basic. It will be found to contain a little more data. This is then recounted. If after two or three repeated recountings of the data, it is still found to be in a low tone, the preclear is told, when returned, that he will remember all this the next time he is brought back to this spot. By advancing him to a happy period and finding that he is then happy, the data is sealed in. After from one to three days, the basic data will be found to have developed to a considerable extent. It is then exhausted again and its behavior noted. If it will not rise easily, many things may be present.

The first thing the auditor should suspect is a precursor. It is actually possible for a follower to contain essential information which will not permit the information to rise. In the course of auditing, when an engram is restimulated by the auditor but will not rise above apathy and does not seem to contain all the necessary data, the auditor must look for a precursor and it almost inevitably will be found to exist. This precursor is then developed as the basic engram. If it follows the same behavior pattern of not lifting or becoming complete, another precursor to it must be discovered. If at last the auditor is entirely certain that there is no engram ahead of the one being cleared, some possible locking mechanism later on may be found and exhausted, at which time the basic may show itself. Continual application of energy to the basic will at length bring it into full view and continual recountings of it will gradually develop it, raise its tone and lift it into Tone 4.

The principle of *recounting* is very simple. The preclear is merely told to go back to the beginning and to tell it all over again. He does this many times. As he does it, the engram should lift in tone on each recounting. It may lose some of its data and gain other. If the preclear is recounting in the same words time after time, it is certain that he is playing a memory record of what he has told you before. He must then be sent immediately back to the actual engram and the somatics of it must be restimulated. He will then be found to somewhat vary his story. He must be returned to the consciousness of somatics continually until these are fully developed, begin to lighten and are then gone. Tone 4 will appear shortly afterward. If the preclear is bored with the incident and refuses to go on with it, there is either a precursor or there is other data in the engram which has not been located.

The auditor will occasionally discover that an engram, when lifted into a Tone 3 (or even erased) without reaching laughter, will *sag*. This is a certain sign of a precursor. Any kind of sag from a Tone 4 is impossible if Tone 4 has truly been reached. Tone 4 will not be reached if there are precursors. The engram may vanish and be erased, but there will be no cheerfulness or laughter about it at the end if it has a precursor.

Once the basic engram has been reached and brought into Tone 4, it will disappear. The next engram on the chain will be located and rather easily brought into Tone 4. If one is accidentally skipped, the third in line will be found to hold or sag. The intermediate must then be located and brought into a Tone 4. In such a way, the engram chain will gradually come up into a complete Tone 4. At this time, it will begin to automatically clear the locks, the merely mentally painful incidents in the person's life. These will clear without any attention from the auditor. While these are clearing, the auditor must concern himself with engram locks. These would be engrams on their own if they had not had precursors. They therefore do not relieve after the removal of the basic, but must be located as themselves. These in turn will start a chain of releasing locks, which again need no attention. There may be entirely distinct engram chains in the reactive mind which are not appended in any way to the original basic engram.

So long as a preclear contains any part of a reactive mind, he will be interested in himself (in the condition of his mind) and introverted. Therefore, so long as he is interested in his own reactive mind, he has engrams. A guarantee of a Tone 4 is the preclear's interest in positive action along his dynamics and his application of himself to the world around him. Introversion is not natural nor is it necessary to the creation of anything. It is a manifestation of the analytical mind trying to solve problems on improper data and observing the organism being engaged in activities which are not conducive to survival in the four dynamics. When a Clear has been reached, the basic personality of the individual will have asserted itself and its self-determinism. No somatics chronic in the present will remain (excepting those which can be accounted for by actual disease, injury or mal-construction of the brain).

Though more germane to Child Dianetics, it is of help to the auditor to know that a child can be considered to have formed his general basic purpose in life somewhere around the age of two. This purpose is fairly reliable as at that time his engrams have probably not gained much force over him, since his responsibilities are slight. He will have tried to hold his main purpose throughout his life, but it will undoubtedly have been warped both by his reactive mind's experience content and by his environment. The discovery of this purpose is obtained by Dianetic revivification and the questioning of the two-year-old child. The time when the purpose is formed varies and may indeed never have manifested, as in the case of amentias. As the preclear is normally interested in this purpose and its rehabilitation, he will often take a more intense interest in therapy if there is an attempt made to discover the purpose. This purpose is quite valid and the preclear can be expected to rehabilitate his life along its dictates unless he is too oppressed by his environment (although it can be remarked that a Clear will ordinarily order or change his environment until he has rehabilitated himself).

Vocational therapies have as their source the tenet of the rehabilitation of the general purpose of an individual or the establishment of a false purpose in order to allay the activity of his reactive mind. It has little bearing on Abnormal Dianetics and belongs more properly in Medical Dianetics, but an auditor, for the term of therapy, may engage his preclear along the purpose line of becoming a Clear. This is not necessary and is indeed often automatic, since the basic personality beholds at last a chance to manifest itself. However, it will occasionally aid the auditor.

The auditor should be prepared to have to solve many individual problems, since above these basics are almost as many problems as there are cases. For example, in the case of a preclear who has several prenatals, it will be found that the formation of the body in the womb has overlaid or confused the time track so that a later prenatal must be partially lifted before an earlier prenatal can be exhausted. This is often true of a later period of life. In one case, an entire series of prenatals was held down by a dental operation under nitrous oxide at the age of twenty-five. Until some portion of the dental operation was removed, the bulk of the prenatals were not available. In short, the circuits of the mind can become entangled to a point where even the motor control time track is confused.

Dispersal of purpose by some engram along some dynamic or purpose line is a common situation and is indeed the basic concept. As a stream of electrons would behave if they were to encounter a solid object in their path, so does a dynamic or purpose disperse. These many varied and faint tracks after impact with the engram are symptomatic. Along Dynamic Two, the sexual dynamic, promiscuity inevitably and invariably indicates a sexual engram of great magnitude. Once that engram is removed, promiscuity can be expected to cease.

Anxiety is established in the preclear's mind by such dispersals and he dramatizes because of the dispersal. This is one of the manifestations of his malady. No pervert ever became a pervert without having been educated or abused by a pervert. And that abuse must have been very thorough.

The contagion of engrams is an interesting manifestation which the auditor should and must observe. It can be said that insanity runs in families, not because this is a eugenic truth, but because a standard patter during emergencies or stress creates certain types of engrams which in turn create types of insanities. Insanities are so definitely contagious that when a child is raised by aberrated parents, he himself becomes aberrated. As would be delineated by Infant and Child Dianetics, the best way to guarantee a sane child is to provide it with Clear parents. This is of definite interest to the auditor, since he will discover that in cases of a severe prenatal and birth, the engrams were also received by the mother exactly as they were received by the child. The child will thereafter be a restimulator to the mother and the mother a restimulator to the child for the severe incidents. The mother, having received the exact wording of the engram, also contains the engram. Restimulation by the child will occasion the use of the engramic language toward the child. This brings the infant and child and adolescent into the unhappy situation of having his birth engram or his prenatal engram continually restimulated. This occasions dire results and very great unhappiness in the home and is one of the main sources of family difficulties.

A child, even if he despises them, will dramatize the actions of his parents when he himself is married and when he himself has children. In addition to this, the other partner in the marriage also has his or her own engrams. Their engrams combine into doubled engrams in the children. The result of this is a contagion and a progression of aberration. Thus, any society which does not have a high purpose finds itself declining and gaining to itself greater numbers of insane. Since the contagion of aberrations is at work progressively, the children become progressively aberrated until at last the society itself is aberrated.

While the fate of society belongs definitely in Social and Political Dianetics, the auditor is interested in the fact that he can take the prenatal and birth content of the engrams of his preclear and run them to discover post-birth locks and engram locks. The mother will normally have used much the same data whenever the troubles of the child impinged upon her reactive mind. This, of course, accounts for the locks.

The auditor will also discover that where he has a married preclear who is aberrated, he should have two preclears, which is to say, the partner. It is useless to return a Clear to his or her aberrated spouse and expect domestic tranquillity to result. While the Clear cannot and will not pick up his old engrams from the spouse in whom he has implanted them, he will nevertheless find his life aberrated by the mere existence of a spouse that he himself may have aberrated.

Further, the children of these people will also need clearing, since they will be found (if the parents' aberrations were of any magnitude) to be sickly or aberrated or deficient in some way. The auditor should therefore, when he undertakes a case, be prepared to assume the family of his preclear, should an investigation of that preclear make it seem necessary.

"Since the contagion of aberrations is at work progressively, the children become progressively aberrated until at last the society itself is aberrated."

Aberrations are contagious and where a person has been aberrated, that environment will to some degree also have become aberrated. The preclear may, for one thing, be somewhat victimized and aberrated by his reactive mind which is now existing in his associates.

The auditor should not permit such terms as "psychoneurotic," "crazy" or "mentally exhausted" to exist for long in the preclear's mind. These are depressant and are actually aberrations in the society. It is true and provable that the preclear is on his way to being, not a person who is crazy or neurotic, but an individual who will have more stability and self-command and ability, possibly, than those around him. To be blunt: this is not the process of reviving corpses into a semblance of life. It is a process which, at its best usage, is taking the "normal" and "average" and giving them their birthright of happiness and creative attainment in the world of Man.

Chapter Thirteen
The Analyzer

The Analyzer

A proper understanding of the approximate working principles of the *analytical mind* is as necessary to the auditor as an understanding of the character and content of the reactive mind.

It can be said, if only for illustration, that the analytical mind is sharply distinct from the remainder of the mind and the body. It can be considered to be the location of the individual's highest echelon in the awareness of "now." In the human being, it is the location of high directional control. In the optimum state of the individual, it possesses the entire self-determinism for the organism. As its energy potential is reduced and its circuits crowded with data of a nonessential nature—which it finds necessary to maintain a continued control, if of a limited extent, of the organism—this determinism is usurped by lower-echelon mechanisms, such as the reactive mind.

The theory of "determinism by stimuli and experience" is true of the lower orders of command mechanisms, as it is in animals. It is distinctly *not* true of the analytical mind. Herein may be said to reside an individual's self-determinism, which is highly selective and self-motivated. It has not only the power of choice in action, it also possesses the ability to create stimuli. It can be considered, for purposes of analogy, as the seat of the four dynamics. Injured or jammed with extraneous data, it chooses to impede various of these dynamics. It has imagination, it can dream, it can create and it is capable of origin in any plane and is capable, additionally, of creating life and matter. Although it may not have done so at this writing, its ability to do so is apparent in enormous progress in that direction. It runs upon the principle that it can solve any problem which it can state. But appreciation of the analytical mind does not depend upon its observed abilities in the creations of a society. It is easily the greatest and most powerful calculator ever known. It can pose itself its own problems and it can invent problems which are far removed from either necessity or observation. It is unlimited. It is a magnificent entity. Billions of words telegraphically composed could not begin to list its achievements and potentials. It is additionally conceived, for brevity in this parity, as being the primary and optimum residence of "I".

Its activity can be delineated by the heuristic axioms of the first chapter. The dynamic and the various dynamics are its only concern.

The analytical mind does not contain engrams. It contains only locks. No pain is residual in the analytical mind beyond a restimulative somatic received in the same manner that it would be received and held by any other organ of the body. The engrams do not intrude into the analytical mind. An entirely different process is observably at work.

By various conduits, the reactive mind is in full command of moments of pain. It is a lower-echelon, immediacy-type mind and can be considered to embrace all the cellular structure of the organism, including the reflexive sub-brains. It runs on exterior determinism and reacts on the plan of A=A=A. It can come into being only when the analytical mind is disorganized or dispersed by exterior forceful means.

The analytical mind may be considered to obtain no direct data from the reactive mind. The entire content of the reactive mind is completely unknown to the analytical mind in any direct fashion. As the analytical mind was not functioning during its receipt, the analytical mind on regaining control of the organism has no connection with the reactive mind.

This single apparent weakness of the analytical mind—that it can be rendered unconscious or dispersed—is a survival mechanism obviously necessary to the organism. There are various reasons for this. It is charged with the command of the dynamics. It cannot consent to the error or injury of the mechanism, which inability is inherent in its primary purpose. It cannot permit the organism to err and when error is introduced, it is the first organ of the body to succumb to extreme shocks. Among others, there is a purely structural reason: shock waves carrying along the nerve channels will disconnect and disrupt the most sensitive nerve area of the body first. Drugs will also produce their maximum effect upon the most sensitive nerve area. The analytical mind is the first affected by shock and drugs. On examination, it will be found to contain fuse mechanisms which preserve it from lasting damage. While it is fantastically sturdy, fantastically able, it is not physiologically stable in the presence of shock or drugs, the latter being, at best, poisons.

The analytical mind has various methods of performing its duties. It can teach itself to think and compute new and outrageously complex methods of computation and then use them to solve problems which it poses to itself, as well as problems which originate in the past, the present or the future environment. It can also originate these environments.

As has been elsewhere noted, its problems may be classified into two groups: obtaining pleasure and solving pain along any one of the four dynamics.

It has nothing to do with the insanity of the organism. It is the first and most interesting case of the contagious character of aberrations. It can control at will any and all portions of the body, any fluid or excretion in the body and, along other dynamics, many other energy forms. To do this, it must solve their menaces and obtain pleasures. It works on observed or imagined data. The imagined or dream data is not aberrated within the analytical mind, but is aberrated data only on the basis of observed reactions. It observes that its charges are in pain. There are five ways in which it can work solutions about that pain. The pain is actual, according to the computations of the analytical mind, when the organism or charges along the other dynamics are observed to be reacting as to a menace and as in pain.

The analyzer is quite adept at throwing out of itself erroneous data. An erroneous datum can only be introduced into a non-pathologic analytical mind by the indirect fact that the pain may not be actual in the organism or other charges. But upon these continually insisting that pain exists, it becomes incumbent upon the analytical mind to bring forth a solution to that pain.

Thus, the content of the analytical mind possesses no direct engram.

The analytical mind does not feel the pain itself unless the pain happens to be in the particular cellular area in which it exists and impinges against its own cellular structure. The "I" is told on certain circuits that the organism is in pain and it observes the fact through sensory perception. In a similar manner, the analytical mind observes that, for instance, a companion individual is injured. It then begins to pose and solve problems regarding that injury. The injury might be non-existent. The companion might only suppose himself to be currently in pain, nevertheless feeling that pain as real. Despite this dissimulation, the analytical mind will endeavor to observe all the data surrounding that pain and to solve the problems relating to it, alleviating it and bettering the companion's present and future chances of survival. A new thought process may be evolved in such a case and the memory of the observation may be stored in the memory banks. This memory contains in itself no actual pain beyond what has been perceived in an analytical fashion.

The reactive mind causes the organism or the entities on other dynamics to simulate pain. In order to enforce engramic commands in a blunt and identity method of survival, portions of the organism or other entities may be made to feel actual pain or may be forcefully limited in food supply or other fluid or necessity service. The exteriorly induced command reacts against the organism or other entities in exactly the pattern and with the perceptics that it was received. The analytical mind is informed on a separate circuit that the organism or other entities are in pain and that it must resolve the problem.

It observes all the surrounding conditions of the incident, or the misery, and with this perfectly valid data, evolves some solution.

The less analytical mind present during such moments, the lower the solution is on its own echelon and the less "rational" that solution will be—which is to say that less computive power has been exerted against the problem. But the entire analytical mind is rational. It is inherently rational. It does not use erroneous data in its computations whenever it is possible to avoid such use. And whenever a datum has been found to be erroneous, the analytical mind discharges the entire circuit of that solution.

When engrams are present in the reactive mind, they come into activation during moments of low potentiality—weariness, drug or trance condition in the analytical mind—but are always to some degree observed by the analytical mind, save when that organ is completely unconscious. Even when only a small amount of the analytical mind's potential is present and the reactive mind is throwing the organism or other entities into aberrated dramatizations, the analytical mind observes, often with incredulity, the action which is taking place. It sees in this action a problem. It attempts to find solutions. And because it is built to resolve solutions on observed as well as conceived data, it soon finds itself in an enormous maze of circuits and complexities which are laid and counter-laid to resolve the problems posed by the dramatization. This observed conduct may be so aberrated that the analytical mind at length finds it necessary to achieve often fantastic solutions. These can include any and all of the insanities. But the analytical mind is never insane, even though it may be nulled for years by the reactive mind and a perceptic which includes the unconsciousness of the analytical mind.

The one common perceptic to all engrams is the dispersal or absence of the analytical mind. They were received at a moment when the analytical mind was unconscious. They therefore contain a datum which states that "when restimulators such-and-so are present, the analytical mind is unconscious." When the analytical mind is low in potentiality or the being low in general tone, it loses some of its control by the simple equation of the comparative energies.

One or more perceptics in an engram being restimulated, a further organic perceptive of "the absence of the analytical mind" is reactivated and circuits are thrown into activity which include a further reduction of the analytical mind. In this way, the analytical mind loses power and command over the organism or the entities it has in its charge.

In a dramatization which includes its suppression or absence, the analytical mind is still in existence, awake and alive in its fullest power, but with all its circuits disengaged as they connect to the body. Insanity is a simple or compound dramatization. Neuroses, compulsions and repressions are the efforts of the analytical mind to reach solutions on observed data with the reactive mind in partial command of the organism. This is not, then, a condition of integration and as many personalities may be posed as there are current dramatizations of engrams in the reactive mind. It is an almost fabulous fact that the analytical mind is constructively and uniformly good in its intent.

To reach the reactive mind, it is necessary to assist the analytical mind so that the reactive personality may be reached. There is, of course, no more actuality in the reactive personality than there is actuality in engrams. These are shadow things, soldered to the body by some painful past experience. This experience includes the partial or complete dispersal of the potential of the analytical mind.

In an insane, neurotic or aberrated individual, it is always possible to lull the reactive mind and reach the slumbering and partially or completely detached and dispersed analytical mind. This presents the remarkable picture of finding within the most "vicious," "criminal" or insane organism, a completely sane, concerned and constructively good *basic personality*. The "I" is never absent but may be disconnected, still trying to solve the problems of the organism or the entities with which it is charged but unable to exert its commands.

The entire intent and technique of Dianetics is to break the partial or complete suppression of the analytical mind by the exhaustion of the false data contained in the engrams which compose the reactive mind. When this is done, the analytical mind begins to clear itself,

"*The entire intent and technique of Dianetics is to break the partial or complete suppression of the analytical mind by the exhaustion of the false data contained in the engrams which compose the reactive mind.*"

somewhat on the order of an automatic computer which makes way for new problems.

Locks are uniformly contained in the analytical mind as observed data. They are therefore reachable in conscious moments in the not-insane individual. Any therapy which addresses the clearing of these locks without consultation with the problem of vanishing the reactive mind is a therapy addressed to a computing mechanism and a powerful "I" far more able to solve problems, if entirely Clear, than any mechanical computer which will ever be built. Freudian psychology, for instance, was an effort to clear the circuits of the analytical mind.

The locks are contained in the analytical mind as notations of confusions observed in the behavior of the organism or the entities which that analytical mind has in its area of observation. These locks are "mental anguish." Anything which addresses the adjustment of them may allay some of the fears of the analytical mind for the organism. But any such effort will be succeeded by new experiences which become locks and must be cleared. That a therapy can be addressed to the analytical mind as a therapy of reason is entirely feasible and possible, for the analytical mind will always receive new data and is quite willing to recompute its old. But its old solutions have become memory of "action undertaken" and are stored additionally in the memory bank so that there are two files. Any therapy addressing the analytical mind does not disturb the memory bank file of locks and these are attached to and will lead to the engram file. But this is an extraordinarily difficult and unnecessary proceeding—to clear the analytical mind of data accumulated by observation. It will produce some alleviation of the analytical mind and even some alleviation of the locks in the memory bank. But it will not and cannot remove the reactive mind unless the engrams themselves are addressed in an orderly and efficient manner.

When the engrams have been exhausted from the reactive mind, all the locks and even some engram locks in the memory banks (and, of course, the analytical mind) vanish, since these depended for their existence upon the charge furnished by the engram, whether bypassed into the memory bank or existing as observation. The analytical mind is very well aware of how the mind works, since it must work not only a mind, but the entire organism and the entities and energy forms included in its dynamics. The moment it observes that the reactive mind has been exhausted and that it is receiving no further pain messages from a certain section which, when restimulated in auditing, were anxiously telegraphing for a solution, it automatically rids itself of all extraneous data and circuits and leaves itself clear for new and rational thought.

Exhaustion of the reactive mind apparently leaves many circuits and much potential in a state of new availability. This is noted in the temporary euphorias which result from the exhaustion of single engrams. This temporary euphoria generally collapses as new engrams are approached in the reactive mind, since the general body tone is reduced and the analytical mind is being confronted with new emergency appeals from various portions of the body.

When the last engram and, where necessary, engramic type of lock is exhausted from the reactive mind and therefore the entire organism and the memory banks, the resultant charge can be compared to a reversed polarity. Laughter is rejection. Violent laughter may often occur as these charges change in the reactive mind and as those circuits are cleared by the analytical mind which is flicking out its locks. The term Clear is used because it is common parlance in the field of computers. The analytical mind, when the reactive mind has been restimulated and exhausted by artificial means, instantly clears itself. This can be considered to make new circuits and computations available. The action does not change in any slightest degree the basic personality of the individual, but delivers to that personality a clear mind relieved of harmful emotional content and an organism which is no longer anxiously telegraphing information about false, but nevertheless real, pain.

It is literally true the analytical mind itself is incapable of error. Its only error is introduced by erroneous data received from its observation of engrams at work. In a Clear, complete accuracy, enormous imagination, renewed dreaming power (since an aberrated individual apparently loses his ability to dream in inverse ratio to the number of engrams he collects) and, above all, the basic dynamic, the four dynamics and purposes are entirely rehabilitated in full force.

The basic purpose of an individual is established at a very early age and is apparently residual in the analytical mind. In a Clear, this purpose comes into full and complete being. His problems no longer have the added complexity of false data—false only in that it was observed as correct, whereas it was false in the reactive mind—and the analytical mind increases markedly in intelligence. It returns to its ability to command the entire organism and the entities which it has in charge and can resolve with fantastic accuracy and speed, modified only by its educational data recallable from the memory files. Discovering the health of the organism to be immeasurably increased, the glandular activity to be normal or returning to normal and the capabilities of the organism to be far in excess of what the organism once supposed they were, the analytical mind can begin with great efficiency to perform its proper function. The happiness and pleasurable observation of life, incident in childhood, comes to the adult with the added enhancement of the ability to concentrate and with the data of long experience. In a Clear, the memory files and the analytical mind contain only valid and useful data and circuits.

Any individual who contains in his reactive mind an experience of an attempted abortion or who contains any engramic data related to the necessity of retaining something, if that suggestion be indefinite, seeks to retain his engrams and will often justify such a retention (since justification for the conduct of the organism is necessary by the analytical mind, which must not permit the organism to remain in social danger) with the comment that "the dynamic results from these engramic situations." The confusion results from the observation that necessity brings about an address of the analytical mind to new problems. The necessities of the past are not forgotten in a Clear, but the false necessities are recognized and eradicated.

It has not been resolved what part punishment plays in the formation of a sensitive analytical mind. But it has been resolved that the removal of the reactive mind, which is to say, the removal of physically painful experience from the life of an individual, immeasurably increases both his dynamic force and his intelligence. The value of a reactive mind to the analyzer is exactly zero.

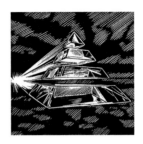

Chapter Fourteen

The Clear

The Clear

The actual operation of the mind, the delineation and measurement of its purposes as well as its dynamics, belongs properly in the field of Dynamic Dianetics. However, the auditor must understand the condition of the *Clear*.

When an individual has had his reactive mind exhausted so that he is no longer victimized by erroneous information, his analytical mind, in which resides the "I", becomes an integration with the entire organism.

As an illustration of this, when the auditor is seeking the basic engram, he will find that the analytical mind (which contains only locks on the engramic content of the reactive mind) will observe that the "I" is exteriorly observing the incident in which the organism once took part until the basic or the basic's immediate chain is reached. This aspect of exterior observation is symptomatic of the disintegrated personality and is present ordinarily in all aberrated individuals until the basic engram itself is reached, at which time the individual will find himself within himself, feeling his own pains and participating as himself in the incident. It was during this basic engram that he first began to separate into the illusion of two or more individuals. In this wise, all aberrated individuals are split personalities, which is to say, unintegrated personalities.

The analytical mind has had its circuits jammed with a great deal of extraneous information and erroneous data furnished by the reactive mind and made to serve as a basic purpose to the analytical mind. These purposes, as furnished by the reactive mind, are of the character of positive suggestions of timeless duration which, when restimulated by perceptions in the environment of the individual, become as new personalities.

Actually, it is not even of interest to the auditor how many personalities the "awake" aberrated individual has assumed or can manifest. In the basic engram, he will find that the personality is integrated, that the individual is within himself. And by following up by careful steps the engram chain, along any and all dynamics, the auditor will continually reintegrate the individual until he is at last in present time as an integrated being—the analytical mind, the "I", being in entire command and possession of the individual. As the analytical mind also contains the basic personality of the individual, for purposes of this illustration, and as that basic personality is good and does obey all the dynamics implicitly and is the personality with which the individual will be most happy and successful, the auditor need pay no attention to the number of times that personality has been split or depressed beyond his initial diagnosis which will permit him to reach the basic engram.

The basic engram is quite locatable, actually, since it will respond very easily to this therapy, in addition to containing the individual as himself, feeling his own pains and consistently within himself throughout the recountings. In an aberrated personality, the basic engram is most usually prenatal and requires considerable patience and development in order to again approach the time track and become available to the analytical mind and so become exhausted.

When he has approached the Tone 4 of the basic personality, or even before he has approached it, the auditor will ordinarily discover that his preclear is beginning to laugh. The laughter will often appear very hysterical, since it is the laughter of relief. Laughter is apparently rejection. And this laughter is the analytical mind finding at length the falsity of the information which it was forced to use in its computations. Not only will the analytical mind force out of its circuits with such laughter all the erroneous information, it will also break automatically all the entirely mentally painful incidents related to that engram or to that engram chain. Even during the breaking of the basic engram, this laughter may often be found to approach the hysterical. This can be explained as a reversal of charge as the analytical mind discovers the unworthiness of the engramic content. After the first engram chain was broken, preclears have been found to laugh for several hours as they were paced up and down their time track looking for locks. These locks often vanish so swiftly they cannot be recounted, such is the power of the analytical mind. The laughter is not necessarily part of the clearing process. But unless laughter is present, the basic engram most certainly has not been reached. If the engram which the auditor considers the basic has been lifted to a certain degree and laughter has not resulted, it is not the basic engram and an earlier incident removed from the time track must be located. So great is the power and fantastic ability of the analyzer—that part of the "I" which can pose to itself its own problems on imaginary environments and evolve entirely original and heretofore unimagined problems and solutions—that it can clear automatically all the future locks from the moment of the engram's receipt without further address by the auditor beyond some prompting with the engramic words.

The Clear is no longer being multi-commanded, but is integrated under the competent command of the basic personality. His analytical mind has had to form various complex, intricate and strange circuits in order to cope with the organism's aberrated belief in the dangers inherent in certain restimulators. As soon as the basic engram has been reached and its immediate chain exhausted, the analytical mind will begin to exhaust itself of all pertinent information and data. Accompanying engrams will achieve a similar result.

The definition of a *Clear* is that he is no longer interested in his own mind. He extroverts rather than introverts. His analytical mind no longer makes errors in simple computations, but can (with its new area which has been released by the locks, thus increasing the intelligence of the individual immeasurably) resolve problems it could not heretofore approach.

The Clear is not the product of destroyed personalities, but is the integration of the very best and the happiest portion of the individual. It is an error to suppose that any personality has been killed. Painful moments in the preclear's life have been exhausted and certain individuals whom the preclear has dramatized, if they were painful to or antagonistic to the individual, are no longer present. But the basic personality is rehabilitated in its fullest and most intelligent and purposeful extent.

The creation of a Clear depends on restoring to the individual his self-determinism. The analytical mind and the "I" are fully capable of self-determinism. The doctrine of "automatic determinism" is false, erroneous and degrading.

The Clear may be interested in clearing other individuals, since that is a portion of his four dynamics. But he will cease to be interested in the condition of his own mind the moment it is smoothly workable and in command of the organism. That mind can then solve the organism's problems in the environment, can solve the environment, can solve the problems of the entities which the organism has in its charge and can, in short, command and create at will.

When an engram has vanished, it can no longer be recalled along the engramic track of the individual and the incident is stored in the memory banks as having been recounted to the auditor.

The character of the Clear is best delineated in the Auditor's Code.

Every individual has his own basic personality and at the age of two has formed his entire purpose for life. The reactive mind has only succeeded in substituting false and detrimental personalities and in warping the purpose of the individual. It has not, in any degree, injured the analytical mind.

Whenever an individual possesses an engram chain which makes the suggestion that he must not get rid of something, he will attempt to hold on to his aberrations. He is reacting solely to an engramic command and is thinking in identities. A Clear is not confused with such matters. For he well recognizes, with the fabulous power of his analyzer, that painfully inflicted exterior determinisms were of no aid to the organism.

Every engram contains the perceptic that the analytical mind must be cut out of the circuit and nullified. This comes about because the engram was received into the reactive mind in moments when great shock or poisons, even when in the form of drugs, deadened or momentarily cut out of the circuit the analytical mind. That the analytical mind can be cut out of the circuit is in itself a survival mechanism, since any organism as sensitive and as complex as the analytical mind must, perforce, be equipped with some fuse mechanism. This then becomes one of the perceptics of organic sensation in any engram. Therefore, when engrams are being dramatized, the analytical mind is instantly lowered in potential even beyond the lowered potential which permitted the engram to become reactive. This is the character of convulsions and so forth. It is therefore possible for some chronically restimulated engram to hold the analytical mind in a suppressed state, such as chronic shock, chronic poisoning or chronic sleep. As these and other things which tend to nullify the analytical mind or reduce its potential are restimulated into dramatization by restimulators in the environment of the individual, the potential of the analytical mind is reduced to a point where it may often appear that the individual is in a chronic trance state. A complete trance of the analytical mind and a chronic restimulation into dramatization of an engram are the commonest forms of insanity. But any series of engrams contains, as part of its restimulative suggestion, the reduction of the analytical mind in its activity. This is a soldered circuit from the engram. Therefore, when a Clear is obtained, the analytical mind is for the first time fully alert. Its circuits are cleared and it can form new thought patterns and can obtain an accuracy of computation which is amazing to watch.

The Clear is the entire being in rationality. He will not harm anything unless rational observation of a situation and the requirements of a society demand that such a thing be harmed.

A Clear is relaxed in a fully conscious state, untroubled by aberrated fears. He is as fully aware of the world around him as an ecstatic child would be and is possessed of a rationality based upon his experience. Painful experience is stored reliably and accurately in his banks as reliable data. But engramic and unconscious experience is eradicated as unreliable and erroneous data.

Freudian psychology addressed the problem of attempting to clear an individual through examining and rationalizing the lock content of the analytical mind. Considerable alleviation may be attempted, after a considerable labor, by any such method. But the engrams still remain and the engrams can still be restimulated, thus forming a new problem for such a therapy. Treatments which tend to blast locks out of the analytical mind, tend to further reduce the dynamics of the individual and destroy the basic personality. For dynamic alone may hold an individual in balance and dynamic alone makes him valuable to himself and his community.

A Clear is rehabilitated in his dynamics and these will be found to be strengthened immeasurably. He is better able to solve the problems of his environment and has available to him more circuits for such computation. He is able to control the organism in its various functions and is an integrated unit. He is rational and constructive. His self-determinism has been rehabilitated to the final degree. And he is no longer subjected to reaction from environmental stimuli, which is characteristic of the base and fumbly animal over which Man has triumphed after fully a million years of evolution.

*"A Clear is rehabilitated in his
dynamics and these will be found to
be strengthened immeasurably."*

Part III

Clearing
DIANETICS: THE ORIGINAL THESIS

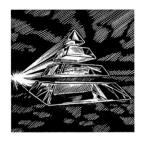

Chapter Fifteen

Engram Chains

Engram Chains

M ore than one *engram chain* will be found in every aberree. When he becomes a preclear, the auditor does well to discover the earliest engram chain. It is not always possible to do this with accuracy since a preclear is sometimes in such a nervous condition that he cannot be worked on his basic chain, but must be alleviated in a greater or lesser degree by the exhaustion of a later and more available chain. This last, however, is not the usual case.

The auditor should clearly understand certain working principles and definitions. By an *engram* is meant a moment of unconsciousness accompanied by physical pain and conceived antagonism. There are two classes of engrams. One is the *basic engram,* which is the earliest engram on an engram chain. The other is the *engram lock,* which is an engram of the same character and kind on the same dynamic as the basic engram of the chain. An *engram chain* is, then, composed of a basic engram and a series of engram locks. Engram chains also contain ordinary *locks,* which are instances of mental anguish more or less known to the analytical mind. These are often mistaken by the preclear for the cause of his conduct. A true engram is unknown to the conscious computer of the preclear, but underlies it as a false datum on which is erected almost equally unknown engram locks and an enormous number of locks.

*"An engram chain is, then, composed of
a basic engram and a series of engram locks."*

In order to release an engram chain, it is vital and absolutely necessary to discover the engrams of that chain. An individual may have more than one engram chain, but he has a *basic engram chain*. This must be cleared as soon as possible after auditing is engaged on the preclear.

When an engram is discovered by the auditor, he must examine the aspect of it to determine whether or not it is the basic. Discovering it is not, he must immediately determine an earlier basic, and so forth, until he is obviously on the scene of the basic engram.

There are certain tests which he can apply. A basic engram will rise to laughter, sag slightly and then rise to Tone 4 and vanish. Successive engrams will then erase from that chain with very little work. Almost any engram on an engram chain can be exhausted. But if it is an engram lock and not a basic engram, it will recede and vanish, at times, but will rise in part again when the basic engram has been reached and the preclear is brought forward into its area.

An engram lock is subject to sag, which is to say that it may be brought to the 2.0 tone, but after a certain length of time has elapsed (from one to two days) it will be found to have sagged and to be, for instance, in a 1.1 tone. It can be successively lifted until it is apparently in a 3.0 tone, at which point much of its content will disappear. This is an *alleviation.*

Any engram chain can be alleviated to some degree without reaching the basic. But when the basic has been reached, the basic itself and subsequent engram locks can be brought rapidly to Tone 4, providing no engram locks are skipped on the return up the time track.

When an engram chain has been brought to Tone 4, it can be considered to have vanished although, while the preclear can no longer find it on the time track (he may even be unable to recall some of its most painful and disheartening aspects), the mind apparently has been proofed against the data it has contained. A search for an engram chain after it has been exhausted and a Tone 4 has been achieved should, for purposes of auditing, be entirely fruitless.

Once the basic has been discovered and the engram chain has been brought to Tone 4, the locks will vanish of their own accord. If this does not occur, then there is something remaining or the auditor has been too optimistic about the selection of his basic engram for the chain and has not, in reality, discovered it.

All engram chains should be exhausted from a preclear. These may be discovered to lie along the various dynamics, but any chain may influence more than one dynamic.

Another type of engram is the *cross-engram*. This is usually a childhood or adult engram which embraces more than one engram chain. The receipt of the cross-engram, containing as it does the convergence of two or more engram chains, is often accompanied by a "nervous breakdown" or the sudden insanity of an individual. A cross-engram may occur in a severe accident, in prolonged or severe illness under antagonistic circumstances or, for instance, in a nitrous oxide operation. Cross-engrams are very easy to locate, but should not be addressed by the auditor, as such, since an enormous amount of work upon them will not exhaust them until the basics and the engram chains on which the cross-engram depends have been brought to Tone 4.

Post-battle neurasthenia is almost always traceable to the receipt of a cross-engram. This must, of course, be an engram in its own right as well as an engram lock on more than one chain. It is conceivable that an engram lock may be so severe that it "breaks" the individual even if it lies on only one engram chain.

There are certain rules the auditor may employ to establish the basic engram of an engram chain. In first entering a case, these rules apply as well to the first goal of the auditor, which is the location of the basic engram of the basic engram chain:

1. No engram will lift if the basic of that chain has not been lifted.

2. The basic engram will not lift until the basic instant of the basic engram has been reached, which is to say, the first moment of the engram. Ordinarily this is the most obscure.

3. If after two or three test recountings of an engram it does not seem to be improving, the auditor should attempt to discover an earlier engram.

4. No engram is valid unless accompanied by somatic pain. This may be mild. Incidents which do not contain somatics are either not basics (the pain having been suspended by some such command as "Can't feel" in the basic) or else it may not even be an engram.

Cases should be entered as near as possible to the basic engram. Then they should be returned to earlier incidents until the basic is discovered.

The treatment of locks themselves may accomplish some alleviation of a case. In view of what can be accomplished by the treatment of engrams, such a gain is not worth consideration by an auditor. Locks should be examined only to discover discrepancies of conduct which will lead to some character of an earlier engram.

Chapter Sixteen

DRAMATIZATION

Dramatization

D*ramatization* is the duplication of an engramic content, entire or in part, in his present time environment by an aberree. Aberrated conduct is entirely dramatization. Aberrated conduct will occur only when and if an engram exists in the reactive mind of the aberree. That conduct will be a duplication of such an engram. The degree of dramatization is in direct ratio to the degree of restimulation of the engrams causing it. A mild dramatization would be a similarity to the engram. A severe dramatization would be an identity with the engram.

When his person is unwearied and he is well and not directly menaced in his environment, the tone level of the entire individual possesses too great a differential from the tone level of the engram, which is always low on the Tone Scale. As the general tone of the individual approaches the tone level of the engram under restimulation, dramatization becomes more severe.

The analytical mind is present to the degree that the general tone of the aberree is high. As this general tone lowers through ill health, reverses or constant restimulation of the reactive mind, the analytical mind is proportionately less aware. Dramatization is demonstrated by the aberree in inverse ratio to the potential of the analytical mind. A geometrical progression is entered, as general tone lowers, to cause the analytical mind to lose its entire awareness potential.

Since every engram contains, as the common denominator of all engrams, the unconsciousness of the organ which is the analytical mind, dramatizations bounce rapidly as this interaction progresses.

In the presence of a relatively high analytical mind awareness potential, dramatization takes the form of similarity. The data of the engram is present, but is interspersed with or modified by justified thought. The physical pain which is always present as part of the dramatization is an equally mild duplication of the pain which was present during the engram. The awareness potential of the analytical mind reduces in the restimulation of the engram, which again reduces the general tone.

The aberree is subject to almost continuous dramatization of one engram or another as the restimulators appear in his vicinity (although the aberration may be so mild as to include only some chronically affected organ). Complete dramatization is complete identity. It is the engram in full force in present time with the aberree taking one or more parts of the dramatis personae present in the engram. He may dramatize all the actors or merely one of them. His dramatization is identity, is unreasoned and always entirely reactive. When the analytical mind reaches the low point of awareness potential it held during the engramic incident, that point is also forced upon the aberree as a part of the dramatization. The aberree may also dramatize himself as he was at the moment of the engram's receipt.

The words, physical actions, expressions and emotions of an aberree undergoing an identity dramatization are those of the single or various dramatis personae present in the engram.

An engram which can be dramatized may, at any time in an aberree's future, be dramatized as an identity dramatization when and if his general tone is low and his environment becomes infiltrated by restimulators.

An aberree, because of high general tone and other factors, may not suffer the restimulation of an engram for a number of years after its receipt. A large number of engrams may be present and undramatized in any aberree if he has never been presented with their particular restimulators in an optimum moment for restimulation.

*"Complete dramatization is complete identity.
It is the engram in full force in present time
with the aberree taking one or more parts of
the dramatis personae present in the engram."*

The common denominator of all insanity is the absence of all, or almost all, awareness potential in the analytical mind. Insanity can be acute or chronic. Any identity dramatization is insanity, by which is meant the entire absence of rationality.

The aberree commonly and chronically dramatizes locks. The engramic content may compel or repress the aberree whenever restimulated.

An irrational person is irrational to the degree that he dramatizes or succumbs to engramic content in his reactive mind. The computations which can be made on the basis of dramatization are infinite. The reactive mind thinks in identities. Dramatizations are severe as they approach identities with the engrams which force them into being in the conduct of the aberree.

The auditor can profit in many ways by these principles of dramatization. By examination of the rage or apathy or hysteria patterns of the preclear, the auditor will find himself in possession of the exact character of the engrams for which he is searching.

In the case of the manic, the fanatic or the zealot, an engram has entirely blocked at least one of the purpose lines deriving from a dynamic. This engram may be called an *assist engram*. Its own surcharge (not the dynamic force) leads the individual to believe that he has a high purpose which will permit him to escape pain. This "purpose" is a false purpose, not ordinarily sympathetic with the organism, having a hectic quality derived from the pain which is part of it even though that pain is not wittingly experienced. This assist engram is using the native ability of the organism to accomplish its false purpose and brings about a furious and destructive effort on the part of the individual who without this assist engram could have better accomplished the same goal. The worst feature of the assist engram is that the effort it commands is engramic dramatization of a particular sort and, if the engram itself is restimulated, the individual becomes subject to the physical pain and fear which the entire experience contained. Therefore, the false purpose itself is subject to sporadic sag. This sag becomes longer and longer in duration between periods of false thrust. It is easy to confuse, in casual observation, an assist engram and an actual valid dynamic unless one also observes the interspersed periods of sag. The assist engram may or may not occasionally accomplish something, but it does accomplish a confusion in the society that the dynamics of the individual are derived from his bad experiences. This is a thing which is emphatically untrue.

Inherently the individual has great willpower. This, however, can be aberrated. Willpower or its absence occasions the attitude of the aberree toward his reactive mind.

The prevention of the dramatization of an engram or a lock further reduces the dynamic of the aberree. Chronic prevention lowers his general tone toward the break point. Unhampered dramatization, as it contains restimulation of a physical pain and the reduced potential of the analytical mind, produces other harmful effects.

Necessity can and does render inactive the entire reactive mind.

Dramatization occurs most often in the absence of necessity or when the reactive mind has obscured the presence of necessity.

Dramatization is residual in the motor controls including speech and can be allayed by the physical exhaustion of the individual. The organism during dramatization tends to revivify toward the moment of the engram's occurrence—the engram containing, as one of its identity parts, the complete physical condition of the organism as at the moment of receiving the engram.

There is no folly or facet of human activity which cannot be dramatized. An immediate alleviation can be achieved when addressing an aberree who is in identity dramatization by acting upon the fact that the conditions of auditing, with one exception, already exist, i.e., the preclear returned to the moment of occurrence. Affinity may be established and Dianetic auditing begun at once. He can be persuaded to listen for the phrases he is uttering and they can be alleviated by exhaustion on routine procedure.

Chapter Seventeen
PRENATAL, BIRTH AND INFANT ENGRAMS

Prenatal, Birth and Infant Engrams

T he human mind and the human anatomy are enormously more powerful and resilient than has commonly been supposed. Only incidents of the greatest magnitude in physical pain and hostile content are sufficient to aberrate a mind.

The ability of the mind to store data can scarcely be overrated. In early life, before sound is analyzed as speech, a human being receives and stores exact impressions of everything which occurs. At some future date, when similar perceptics are encountered, the reactive mind re-analyzes—on the basis of identities only—the content of the early mind. This becomes the foundation of the post-conception personality. The actual personality in the individual is powerful and very difficult to aberrate. Unlike animals, which can be driven mad by minor mechanisms of experimental psychology, a man must be most severely handled before he begins to show any signs of derangement. That derangement proceeds from the ability of the reactive mind to store perceptions from the earliest moments of existence and retain them on either the analytical or the reactive plane for future reference.

The basic personality does not proceed from engrams. And the dynamics of the individual are impeded, not enhanced, by engrams. The dynamics are entirely separate and are as native to the individual as his basic personality, of which they are a part.

Information falls into two categories: the *educational,* or experience level, banked and available to the analytical mind on at least its deeper levels; and *aberrational,* or data stored in the reactive mind and often used by, but never reached by, the analytical mind (save through auditing).

There would seem to be two types of recording. The first is cellular recording in which the cells would seem to store data. In that cells in procreating become themselves again (which is to say that when cell A divides, both halves are still cell A), cellular intelligence is not lost, personal identity is duplicated. In the case of individual men, procreation is far more complex and individual identity is lost—the son is not the father, but a genetic composite of vast numbers of ancestors.

The cells of the human being shortly after conception are capable of enormous perceptic and retentive power. After a very short time in the womb, the brain and nervous system are already operating. From then until birth, the human being is apparently capable of computations of a rather complex nature on the analytical-mind level. Far more certainly, he retains information on the reactive level.

Fear, pain and unconsciousness extend the range of perception of the individual. When the human being in the womb is injured, his senses extend so as to record sounds outside the mother's body. He records them so well that their precise nature is stored for future reference. The human being in the womb responds exactly as it does after birth to the receipt of engrams, storing the data with precision and reacting to it.

The repair facilities available to a human being before birth are greatly enhanced by the presence of ample connective tissue, oxygen and sustenance. These repair facilities are unimaginably great, so that a prenatal human being can be severely torn and ripped without becoming structurally deficient. It does, however, receive engrams and these engrams are subject to restimulation. In many cases of attempted abortions, it was found that large sections of the prenatal human being's brain could apparently be injured without the brain being deficient or even scarred after birth. These repair facilities do not, however, lessen the extreme severity of the engrams which can be received by the prenatal human being. The word "fetus" is dropped at this point and it is advised that it should be dropped from the language as a description of a pre-birth human being. Insufficient evidence is at hand to make an outright declaration that attempted abortions are responsible for the bulk of our criminal and insane aberrees. But according to the cases at hand, the attempted abortion must be accounted responsible for the majority.

The attempted abortion is the most serious aberration producer. So exact is the recording of the pre-birth human being, or *prenatal,* that the reactive mind makes no errors in recognizing its enemies after birth. The mind becomes aberrated in having to depend upon these same enemies for the ordinary sustenance of life while the child is a helpless infant.

The diagnosis of a prenatal case is relatively simple. Nearly all preclears will be found to have at least one prenatal engram and the case will not solve unless that prenatal is reached and exhausted.

The auditor can usually establish the attempted abortion preclear by an investigation of the conduct of the infant and child. Uneasiness or unhappiness in the home, a feeling of not being wanted, unreasonable fear and a strong attachment to grandparents or another non-parental member of the household are often signs of an attempted abortion. Fear of the dark is usually, but not always, a part of the attempted abortion case. The auditor should suspect an abortion attempt in every preclear he audits, at least for this next generation. Whether or not the preclear disbelieves the diagnosis is of no importance to the auditor as the prenatal engrams may very well contain the words "Can't believe it." The parents themselves, as well as society, mislead the individual as to the enormous prevalence at this time of this practice.

The attempted abortion preclear may not be discovered to be such until considerable auditing has already been done. Any auditing done on an attempted abortion preclear, unless it is solely addressed to making the case workable, is wasted until the attempted abortions are reached. The post-birth aberree presents a somewhat different case than the prenatal, since his case can be entered at any point and the earliest moments of it can be attained easily. This is not true of the attempted abortion preclear. Attempted abortions may run to any number, since they are easily the most prevalent dramatization of engram in the society. They are repeated time and again.

The auditor will find it necessary to "unstack" the prenatal period. He will ordinarily reach the latest prenatal injury first. As he finds and examines it, it places itself on the time track. By continuous returning to earlier and earlier attempts, more and more of these engrams are revealed until at last the earliest is discovered. The auditor must be prepared to spend many hours of hard work in unstacking injuries. He will many times believe that he has reached the basic of that engram chain, only to discover that another type of abortion was attempted prior to that moment. He need not address these engrams for any length of time before he goes on to the earlier one. He should only get some idea of them so that they will be easily locatable on the return.

The basic engram on the attempted abortion case may be found shortly after the first missed period of the mother. Its emotion will be exactly that of the person or persons attempting to perform the abortion. The prenatal human being identifies himself with himself, but an adult returned to the prenatal period is reinterpreting the data and will find that he has and is confusing himself with other people associated in the attempts. This engramic data may have slumbered for years before it became violently restimulated and may, indeed, never have been awakened. It must be removed, however, before a Clear can be obtained. The auditor should be prepared to unstack fifty or more incidents before birth if necessary.

When he is at last in the vicinity of the basic, even the most skeptical preclear (one who has skepticism as part of the prenatal engram chains) will have no further question as to what is happening to him. The auditor should be prepared to encounter difficulty in the ability of the preclear to hear voices or feel pain as it is quite common for the engramic content to contain such phrases as "Unconscious" and "Can't see, can't feel, can't hear," this having been the misconception of the society regarding prenatal life.

The auditor should never be appalled at the damage the prenatal human being has received and so question the validity of his preclear's data. Unless the umbilical cord is severed or the heart is stopped, it is apparently the case that no damage, particularly in the earlier months, is too great for the organism to reconstruct.

In that parents performing abortions are usually dramatizing attempted abortions which have been performed on them, rationality of content in the engrams should not be expected. Even the data given for it by the abortionists—father, mother or professional—is often entirely inaccurate.

The test of an engram is whether or not it will lift and whether or not the somatics which accompanied it disappear and a Tone 4 is obtained. Rearranging data into other sequences will not obtain this. The exact content must be brought out. If the prenatal human being's recording mechanism was so disturbed that it did not, at some period in the attempt, record, then there is no engram for the blank period only. But this is a theoretical case only; there has not been one yet discovered.

The attempted abortion human being is often struck unconscious by the earliest part of each attempt, since the head is so available to the knitting needles, hatpins, orangewood sticks, buttonhooks and so forth which are employed. These periods of unconsciousness must be penetrated and will quite ordinarily release slowly.

The number of prenatal engrams should not particularly appall the auditor, for when the basic has been discovered and a Tone 4 achieved, the succeeding experiences will lift with greater and greater ease. The periods of unconsciousness interspersed between the prenatal engrams, being locks, will vanish.

Birth is in itself a severe experience and is recorded by the human being from the first moments of pain throughout the entire experience. Everything in a birth is engramic, since the human being conceives the ministrations to be more or less antagonistic since they are accompanied by so much pain. A birth must be lifted as a matter of course, but not until the presence or absence of prenatals has been established. Even after birth has been lifted, prenatals should be looked for, since prenatals may often be found only after birth has been exhausted. The habits of obstetricians, the presence of sound and speech in the delivery room, the swabbing of an infant's nostrils, the examination of its mouth, the severe treatment administered to start its breathing and the drops in the eyes may account in themselves for many psychosomatic ills. A cough, however, although it is present in birth and seems to be alleviated by the exhaustion of the birth engram, is quite ordinarily blood running down the throat of the prenatal during an attempted abortion. Any perception during birth, when difficulty is encountered with breathing, may become a restimulator for asthma. Clean fresh air and electric lights may cause allergies and may be the principal restimulators. Everything said during birth as well as everything said during prenatal engrams is recorded in the reactive mind and acts as aberrational matter which can and does cause psychological and physiological changes in the individual. Because the parents are not greatly in evidence at birth, this experience may not be restimulated for many years. Prenatals, on the other hand, restimulate more easily.

Infant life is very sentient. Delay in learning to talk is delay in learning the complexity of handling vocal muscles rather than a delay in ability to record. Everything in infant life is recorded and the engrams received in it are extremely valid.

The auditor will find himself dealing mainly with prenatal, birth and infant life. The cases are very rare which have many important basics in childhood or adult life. These last periods contain mainly engram locks which, though they must be addressed to create the Clear, should not engage much initial attention on the part of the auditor. Most of the experiences of mental anguish in childhood and adult life are founded on very early engrams and are locks which are self-removing.

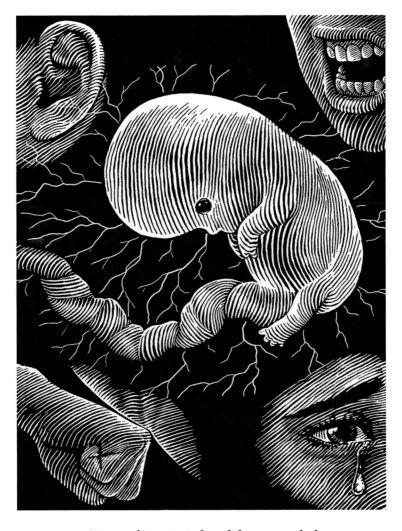

"Everything in infant life is recorded
and the engrams received in it are extremely valid.
The auditor will find himself dealing mainly with
prenatal, birth and infant life. The cases are
very rare which have many important basics
in childhood or adult life."

Moments of unconsciousness which contain physical pain and conceived antagonism lying in childhood and adult life are serious and can produce aberration. Engram chains complete with basic may be found which will, all by themselves, exhaust. But little if any actual aberration comes after the fifth year is reached.

Chapter Eighteen
The "Laws" of Returning

The "Laws" of Returning

By *aberration* is meant the preclear's reactions to and difficulties with his current environment.

By *somatic* is meant any physical or physically sensory abnormality which the preclear manifests generally or sporadically in his environment, or any such manifestation encountered and re-experienced in the process of auditing.

The aberration is the mental error caused by engrams and the somatic is the physical error occasioned by the same source.

The auditor follows the general rule that no aberrations or somatics exist in a preclear which cannot be accounted for by engrams. He may ordinarily be expected to discover that anything which reduces the physical or mental perfection of the preclear is engramic. He applies this rule first and in practice admits no organic trouble of any character. Only when he has obviously obtained a Clear and when he has observed and medically examined that Clear, after a period of sixty days to six months from end of auditing, should he be content to assign anything to organic origin. He cannot be expected to know until the final examination exactly what somatic was not engramic. In other words, he must persistently adhere to one line of thought (that the preclear can be brought to mental and physical perfection) before he resigns any mental or physical error in the preclear to a purely organic category.

Too little is known at this writing of the recoverability of the mind and body for an auditor to deny that ability to recover. Since primary research, considerable practice has demonstrated that this ability to reconstruct and recover is enormous, far beyond anything previously conceived possible.

Dianetics accounts for *all* faith healing phenomena on an entirely scientific basis and the auditor can expect himself to consort daily in his practice with what appear to be miracles.

In addition to knowledge of his subject, considerable intelligence and imagination and a personality which inspires confidence, the auditor must possess persistency to a remarkable degree. In other words, his dynamics must be phenomenally high. There is no substitute for the auditor having been cleared. It is possible for an individual to operate with Dianetics without having been cleared and he may do so for some time without repercussion. But as he practices, he will most certainly encounter the perceptics contained in some of his own engrams, time after time, until these engrams are so restimulated that he will become mentally or physically ill.

In psychoanalysis, it was possible for the analyst to escape this fate because he dealt primarily with locks occurring in the post-speech life. The analyst might even experience relief from operating on patients, since it might clarify his own locks which are (and more or less always had been) completely available to his analytical mind. This is very far from the case with the auditor who handles continually the vital and highly charged data which *cause* physical and mental aberrations. An auditor in Dianetics may work with impunity for a very short time only before his own condition demands that he himself be cleared of his engrams. While this is aside from the main subject of auditing, it has been too often observed to be neglected.

Every engram possesses some quality which denies it to the analytical mind. There are roughly four types of denial. First there is the *self-locking* engram, which contains the species of phrases "Frank will never know about this" "Forget it!" "Cannot remember it" and so forth.

Second is the *self-invalidating* engram, which contains the species of the phrases "Never happened" "Can't believe it" "Wouldn't possibly imagine it" and so on.

Third is the *preclear-ejection* engram, which contains the species of phrases "Can't stay here" "Get out!" and other phrases which will not permit the preclear to remain in its vicinity, but return him to present time.

The fourth is the *preclear-seizing* engram, which contains the species of phrases "Stay here" "Hold still" "Can't get out" and so on.

These four are the general types which the auditor will find to occasion him the greatest difficulty. The type of phrase being encountered, however, is easily diagnosed from preclear reaction.

There are many other types of engrams and species of phrases which will be encountered. There is the self-perpetuating engram which implies that "It will always be this way" and "It happens all the time." The auditor will soon learn to recognize them, forming lists of his own.

An engram would not be an engram unless it had strong compulsive or repressive data contained in it. All engrams are self-locking to some degree, being well off the time track and touching it slightly, if at all, with some minor and apparently innocuous bit of information which the analytical mind disregards as unimportant. Classed with the self-locking specific variety are those phrases which deny perception of any kind. The auditor will continually encounter perception denial and will find it one of the primary reasons the preclear cannot recall and articulate the engram. "Can't see" "Can't hear" "Can't feel" and "Isn't alive" tend to self-lock the whole engram containing any such phrases.

As the engram is a powerful surcharge of physical pain, it will, without any phrases whatsoever, deny itself to the analytical mind which in seeking to scan it is repelled by its operating principle that it must avoid pain for the organism. As has already been covered, there are five ways the organism can handle a source of pain. It can neglect it, attack it, succumb to it, flee from it or avoid it.

As the entire organism handles exterior pain sources, so does the analytical mind tend to react to engrams. There is an exterior-world reaction of the organism to pain sources, then. This is approximated when the analytical mind is addressed in regard to engrams. There is an excellent reason for this. Everything contained in the reactive mind is exterior-source material. The analytical mind was out of circuit and was recording imperfectly, if at all, in the time period when the exterior source was entered into the reactive mind.

An analytical mind, when asked to approach an engram, reacts as it would have had it been present, which is to say, out of circuit at the moment when the engram was being received. Therefore, an approach to the engram must be made which will permit the auditor to direct the preclear's analytical mind into but one source of action: Attack.

The actual incident must be located and re-experienced. In that the analytical mind has five possible ways of reacting to the engram and in that the auditor desires that only one of these—attack—be used, the preclear must be persuaded from using the remaining four.

On this general principle can be created many types of approach to the problem of obtaining a Clear. The one which is offered in this manual is that one which has met with quicker and more predictable results than others researched. It has given, in use, 100 percent results in obtaining Clears. In the beginning, at this time, an auditor should not attempt to stray far from this offered technique. He should attempt to vary it only when he himself has had extensive and sufficient practice which will enable him to be very conversant with the nature of engrams. Better techniques will undoubtedly be established which will provide swifter exhaustion of the reactive mind.* The offered technique has produced results in all types of cases so far encountered.

There are three equations which demonstrate how and why the auditor and preclear can reach engrams and exhaust them:

---

*See *Dianetics: The Modern Science of Mental Health,* the complete handbook of Dianetic procedure.

I.   THE AUDITOR'S DYNAMICS ARE EQUAL TO OR LESS THAN THE ENGRAMIC SURCHARGE IN THE PRECLEAR.

II. THE PRECLEAR'S DYNAMICS ARE LESS THAN THE ENGRAMIC SURCHARGE.

III. THE AUDITOR'S DYNAMICS PLUS PRECLEAR'S DYNAMICS ARE GREATER THAN THE ENGRAMIC SURCHARGE.

When the preclear's dynamics are entirely or almost entirely reduced, the auditor's dynamics are not always sufficient to force the preclear's analytical mind into an attack upon the engram.

The auditor's dynamics directed against an engram in a preclear who has not been subjected to a process which will inhibit the free play of his reactive mind and concentrate it, ordinarily provokes the preclear into one of the four unusable methods of succumbing, fleeing, avoiding or neglecting the engram. Demanding that the preclear "face reality," or "see reason," or that he "stop his foolish actions" fall precisely into this category. The auditor's dynamics operating against a preclear can produce a "break," temporary or of considerable duration, in the preclear.

When the preclear is in reverie, some of his own dynamics are present and the auditor's dynamics *added* to these make a combination sufficient to overcome the engramic surcharge.

If the auditor releases his dynamics *against* the analytical mind of the preclear, which is to say, the person of the preclear, while an attempt is being made to reach an engram (in violation of the Auditor's Code or with some erroneous idea that the whole person of the preclear is confronting him), the auditor will receive in return all the fury of the engramic surcharge.

An engram can be dramatized innumerable times, for such is the character of the reactive mind that the surcharge of the engram cannot exhaust itself and will not exhaust itself, regardless of its age or the number of times dramatized, until it has been approached by the analytical mind of the preclear.

"I. The auditor's dynamics are equal to or less than the engramic surcharge in the preclear.

II. The preclear's dynamics are less than the engramic surcharge.

III. The auditor's dynamics plus preclear's dynamics are greater than the engramic surcharge."

The additive dynamic law must be made to apply before engrams are reached. It is very occasionally necessary to change Dianetic auditors, for some preclears will work well only with either a male or a female auditor or with one or another individual auditor. This will not be found necessary in many cases. Three cases are on record where the preclear was definitely antipathetic toward the auditor throughout the entire course of auditing. The auditor was found to be a restimulator for one or more of the persons contained in the engrams. Even so, these people were cleared. Greater patience was required on the part of the auditor, closer observance of the Auditor's Code was necessary and a longer time was required for auditing. It will be discovered that once the preclear understands what is desired of him and why, his basic personality is aroused to the extent that it will cooperate with any auditor in order to be free. It will suffer through many violations of the Auditor's Code. Once a preclear has been entered upon auditing, he will ordinarily continue to cooperate in the major requirements to the fullest extent, no matter what apparent antagonisms he may display in minor matters.

The fact that the auditor is interested solely in what has been done *to* the preclear and is not at all interested in what the preclear himself has done to others greatly facilitates therapy, since there is no social disgrace in having been an unwitting victim.

The preclear is placed in a light state of "concentration," which is not to be confused with hypnosis. In the state of alliance, therefore, the mind of the preclear will be found to be to some degree detachable from his surroundings and directed interiorly. The first thing that the auditor will discover in most preclears is aberration of the sense of time. There are various ways that he can circumvent this and construct a time track along which he can cause the preclear's mind to travel. Various early experiences which are easily reached are examined and an early diagnosis can be formed. Then begins an immediate effort to reach basic, with attempted abortion or prenatal accident predominating. Failures on the first attempts to reach prenatal experiences should not discourage the auditor, since many hours may be consumed and many false basics reached and exhausted before the true prenatal basic is attained.

The auditor can use and will observe certain apparently natural laws in force. They are as follows:

1. The difficulties the analytical mind encounters when returned to or searching for an engram are identical to the command content of that engram.

2. A preclear in adult life is more or less obeying, as restimulated, the composite experiences contained in his engrams.

3. The preclear's behavior in returning is regulated by the commands contained in the engram to which he is returned and is modified by the composite of chronologically preceding engrams on his time track.

4. The somatics of a preclear are at their highest in an engram where they were received and at the moment of reception in that experience.

5. When returned prior to an engram, the commands and somatics of that engram are not effective on the preclear. As he is returned to the moment of an engram, the preclear experiences, as the common denominator of all engrams, a considerable lessening of his analytical potential. He speaks and acts in a modified version of the engram. All complaints he makes to the auditor should be regarded as possibly being verbatim from: first, the engram that he is re-experiencing; or second, from prior engrams.

6. At the precise moment of an engramic command, the preclear experiences obedience to that command. The emotion a preclear experiences when returned to an engram is identical to the emotional tone of that engram. Excesses of emotion will be found to be contained in the word content of the engram as commands.

7. When a preclear is returned before the moment of reception of an engram, he is not subject to any part of that engram emotionally, aberrationally or somatically.

8. When the time track is found to contain "loops" or is blurred in any of its portion, its crossings or confusions are directly attributable to engramic commands which precisely state the confusion.

9. Any difficulty a preclear may experience with returning, reaching engrams, perceiving or recounting are directly and precisely commanded by engrams.

10. An engram would not be an engram were it easy to reach, gave the preclear no difficulty and contained no physical pain.

11. The characteristic of engrams is confusion: first, the confusion of the time track; second, the confusion of an engram chain wherein similar words or somatics mix incidents; third, confusion of incidents with engrams. This confusion is occasioned by the disconnected state of the analytical mind during the receipt of the engram.

12. Auditing, by location and identification of hidden incidents: first, rebuilds at least the early part of the time track; locates and fixes engrams in relation to one another in time; and then, locates the basic of the basic chain and exhausts it. The remainder of the chain must also be exhausted. The engram locks exhaust with ease after the erasure of the basic engram or the basic of any chain (within that chain). Locks vanish without being located. A Tone 4 gained on basic permits the subsequent erasure on the time track to go forward with ease. A whole chain may rise to 4 without the basic chain having been located.

13. Any perception of pre-speech life during returning connotates the existence of engramic experience as far back as the time track is open.

14. If the individual's general tone is not clearly Tone 4, if he is still interested in his engrams, another more basic chain than the one found still exists.

15. Engram patterns tend to form an avoidance pattern for the preclear. From basic outward, there is an observable and progressive divergence between the preclear himself and his returned self. In the basic engram of the basic chain and for a few subsequent engrams on that chain, he will be found within himself and receiving the experiences as himself. In subsequent engrams, cleavage is observable. And in late engrams, the preclear is found to be observing the action from the outside of himself, almost as a disinterested party. This forms the principal primary test for the basic of the basic chain.

16. Another test for basic is sag. Any engram may be exhausted to a point where it will recede without reaching Tone 4. Although it is temporarily and momentarily lost to the individual and apparently does not trouble him, that engram which has been exhausted in a chain without the basic having been reached will sag or reappear within twenty-four to sixty hours. Basic on any chain will not sag, but will lift on a number of recountings, rise to Tone 4 and will remain erased.

17. Another test for basic is whether or not it begins to lift with ease. If an engram does not intensify or remain static after many recountings, it can be conceived to be at least a basic on some engram chain.

18. Locks will lift and disappear without returning as they are not fixed in the body by physical pain. Large numbers of locks can be exhausted, bringing an alleviation of the preclear's difficulties, and such a course may occasionally be pursued in the entrance of a case. The discovery and lifting of the basic to which the locks are appended removes the locks automatically.

These rules and laws, unless modified in their statement, will be found invariable. Incompetent auditing cannot be excused by the supposed discovery of a special case or exception. A physical derangement must be in the category of actually missing parts of the organism to cause permanent disability and instances of this are not common.

LRH Glossary

LRH Glossary

DIANETICS:

Derived from the Greek word for thought, *dianoia.* A term employed to embrace the science of thought and including a family of sub-sciences by which the individual and collective activities of Mankind may be understood and predicted and bettered.

ABNORMAL DIANETICS:

That branch of Dianetics which includes the axioms and processes of the science which treats the aberrated mind, including all techniques necessary to the alleviation or cure of such aberrations and establishing a Tone 4 in the individual. It does not embrace the study of those who are insane through anatomical deficiencies or through injury. These are a subject for research under Dynamic Dianetics.

DYNAMIC DIANETICS:

The science of the basic dynamics of the individual and his basic personality. At this writing, that branch of Dianetics most intensely under observation and research is this one.

TONE:

The emotional condition of an engram or the general condition of an individual.

DYNAMIC:

The dynamic thrust into time and space of an individual, a species, or a unit of matter or energy. Especially defined, for the purpose of Dianetics, as "Survive!"

PURPOSE:

The survival route chosen by an individual, a species or a unit of matter or energy in the accomplishment of its Dynamic. (Note: The purpose is specific and may be closely defined being a subdivision of one of the sub-dynamics. It has been tentatively established by investigation that an individual human being has established his purpose for life at the age of two years and that the actual purpose is not derived in any degree from engrams, but is only warped by them.)

ENGRAM:

A period of physical pain including unconsciousness and antagonism experienced by an individual, group or society and residing thereafter as irrational and restimulatable dramatizations.

ENGRAM LOCK:

An engram, severe in its own right, succeeding a basic engram on any engram chain.

ENGRAM CHAIN:

A series of similar engrams on one or more dynamics which impede the dynamics of the individual.

Lock:

A period of mental anguish depending for its force upon an engram. It may or may not be available to the analytical mind, but it does not contain actual unconsciousness.

Dispersal:

The action of a dynamic or purpose meeting an engram. It is describable by an analogy of an electron stream striking impedance and showering around it, much weakened.

Confusion:

The condition of an area of an engram or the condition of an engram chain. Instants of existence which are not properly aligned on the time track.

Time Track:

The memory record of an individual, motor or sensory, is precisely aligned on moments of time. In a Clear, all such moments are available to the analytical mind. In an aberree, areas of the time track are obscured, but the time track is considered to be in perfect condition, if partially and temporarily obscured. The existence of two time tracks is suspected—one sensory and one motor, the latter being more available to the auditor in the form of somatics. The time track is precise, but as the analytical mind addresses it in the aberree it is apparently obliterated in part or tangled.

Preclear:

Any individual entered upon Dianetic therapy for the purpose of being cleared.

Dianeticist:

An auditor of Dianetic therapy.

ABERREE:

An aberrated individual, sane or insane, containing unrelieved engrams.

CLEAR:

An individual who has been cleared of all engrams and engram chains and who has achieved a general Tone 4.

AA:

An attempted abortion case.

CROSS-ENGRAM:

The severe engramic experience wherein two engram chains have met, causing a marked change in the life of the individual. This is an engram which is on the time track of each of two or more chains.

BREAK ENGRAM:

The engram lock after the receipt of which the individual experienced a lowering of general tone to 2.5 or less and became therefore unable to cope with his environment.

TRAUMA:

A term from a school of psychology implying an experience which would create a psychic scar. It is unused in Dianetics as being liable to misunderstanding of the nature of severe experiences. Scars cannot be removed; psychosomatic experiences can be.

RESTIMULATOR:

The environmental perceptic which approximates a precise part of the engramic perceptics in the reactive mind.

Associative Restimulator:

A perceptic in the environment which is confused with an actual restimulator.

Reactive Mind:

That portion of the mind which contains reflexive or reactive data which does not clear through the analytical mind, but is subject to dramatization or aberration. It uses as a thought process the conception of identities: A=A=A. This is essentially the animal thinking mechanism.

Analytical Mind:

The residence of consciousness in the individual and the seat of his dynamics and basic personality. This is an analogical term. The analytical mind can be subdivided.

Unconsciousness:

A period of cessation of activity on the part of the analytical mind only. The reactive mind is active and is conscious in the majority of his being, in all degrees of life, no matter how nearly approaching death. (This is a condition of the total individual in death only.)

Somatic:

The physiological counterpart of mental aberration. A somatic attends every aberration. This term is used in lieu of "physical pain" in therapy, due to the high engramic value of the word "pain" and its failure to include in its meaning all painful perceptics.

Appendix

Further Study
Books & Lectures by L. Ron Hubbard

The materials of Dianetics and Scientology comprise the largest body of information ever assembled on the mind, spirit and life, rigorously refined and codified by L. Ron Hubbard through five decades of research, investigation and development. The results of that work are contained in hundreds of books and more than 3,000 recorded lectures. A full listing and description of them all can be obtained from any Scientology Church or Publications Organization. (See *Guide to the Materials*.)

The books and lectures below form the foundation upon which the Bridge to Freedom is built. They are listed in the sequence Ron wrote or delivered them. In many instances, Ron gave a series of lectures immediately following the release of a new book to provide further explanation and insight of these milestones. Through monumental restoration efforts, those lectures are now available and are listed herein with their companion book.

While Ron's books contain the summaries of breakthroughs and conclusions as they appeared in the developmental research track, his lectures provide the running day-to-day record of research and explain the thoughts, conclusions, tests and demonstrations that lay along that route. In that regard, they are the complete record of the entire research track, providing not only the most important breakthroughs in Man's history, but the *why* and *how* Ron arrived at them.

Not the least advantage of a chronological study of these books and lectures is the inclusion of words and terms which, when originally used, were defined by LRH with considerable exactitude. Far beyond a mere "definition," entire lectures are devoted to a full description of each new Dianetic or Scientology term—what made the breakthrough possible, its application in auditing as well as its application to life itself. As a result, one leaves behind no misunderstoods, obtains a full conceptual understanding of Dianetics and Scientology and grasps the subjects at a level not otherwise possible.

Through a sequential study, you can see how the subject progressed and recognize the highest levels of development. The listing of books and lectures below shows where *Dianetics: The Original Thesis* fits within the developmental line. From there you can determine your *next* step or any earlier books and lectures you may have missed. You will then be able to fill in missing gaps, not only gaining knowledge of each breakthrough, but greater understanding of what you've already studied.

This is the path to knowing how to know, unlocking the gates to your future eternity. Follow it.

DIANETICS: THE ORIGINAL THESIS • *(This current volume.)* Ron's *first* description of Dianetics. Originally circulated in manuscript form, it was soon copied and passed from hand to hand. Ensuing word of mouth created such demand for more information, Ron concluded the only way to answer the inquiries was with a book. That book was Dianetics: The Modern Science of Mental Health, now the all-time self-help bestseller. Find out what started it all. For here is the bedrock foundation of Dianetic discoveries: the *Original Axioms,* the *Dynamic Principle of Existence,* the *Anatomy of the Analytical* and *Reactive Mind,* the *Dynamics,* the *Tone Scale,* the *Auditor's Code* and the first description of a *Clear.* Even more than that, here are the primary laws describing *how* and *why* auditing works. It's only here in Dianetics: The Original Thesis.

DIANETICS: THE EVOLUTION OF A SCIENCE • This is the story of *how* Ron discovered the reactive mind and developed the procedures to get rid of it. Originally written for a national magazine—published to coincide with the release of Dianetics: The Modern Science of Mental Health—it started a wildfire movement virtually overnight upon that book's publication. Here then are both the fundamentals of Dianetics as well as the only account of Ron's two-decade journey of discovery and how he applied a scientific methodology to the problems of the human mind. He wrote it so you would know. Hence, this book is a must for every Dianeticist and Scientologist.

DIANETICS: THE MODERN SCIENCE OF MENTAL HEALTH • The bolt from the blue that began a worldwide movement. For while Ron had previously announced his discovery of the reactive mind, it had only fueled the fire of those wanting more information. More to the point—it was humanly impossible for one man to clear an entire planet. Encompassing all his previous discoveries and case histories of those breakthroughs in application, Ron provided the complete handbook of Dianetics procedure to train auditors to use it everywhere. A bestseller for more than half a century and with tens of millions of copies in print, Dianetics: The Modern Science of Mental Health has been translated in more than fifty languages, and used in more than 100 countries of Earth—indisputably, the most widely read and influential book about the human mind ever written. And that is why it will forever be known as *Book One.*

DIANETICS LECTURES AND DEMONSTRATIONS • Immediately following the publication of *Dianetics,* LRH began lecturing to packed auditoriums across America. Although addressing thousands at a time, demand continued to grow. To meet that demand, his presentation in Oakland, California, was recorded. In these four lectures, Ron related the events that sparked his investigation and his personal journey to his groundbreaking discoveries. He followed it all with a personal demonstration of Dianetics auditing—the only such demonstration of Book One available. *4 lectures.*

DIANETICS PROFESSIONAL COURSE LECTURES—*A SPECIAL COURSE FOR BOOK ONE AUDITORS* • Following six months of coast-to-coast travel, lecturing to the first Dianeticists, Ron assembled auditors in Los Angeles for a new Professional Course. The subject was his next sweeping discovery on life—the *ARC Triangle,* describing the interrelationship of *Affinity, Reality* and *Communication.* Through a series of fifteen lectures, LRH announced many firsts, including the *Spectrum of Logic,* containing an infinity of gradients from right to wrong; *ARC and the Dynamics;* the *Tone Scales of ARC;* the *Auditor's Code* and how it relates to ARC; and the *Accessibility Chart* that classifies a case and how to process it. Here, then, is both the final statement on Book One Auditing Procedures and the discovery upon which all further research would advance. The data in these lectures was thought to be lost for over fifty years and only available in student notes published in Notes on the Lectures. The original recordings have now been discovered making them broadly available for the first time. Life in its highest state, *Understanding,* is composed of Affinity, Reality and Communication. And, as LRH said, the best description of the ARC Triangle to be found anywhere is in these lectures. *15 lectures.*

SCIENCE OF SURVIVAL—*PREDICTION OF HUMAN BEHAVIOR* • The most useful book you will ever own. Built around the *Hubbard Chart of Human Evaluation,* Science of Survival provides the first accurate prediction of human behavior. Included on the chart are all the manifestations of an individual's survival potential graduated from highest to lowest, making this the complete book on the Tone Scale. Knowing only one or two characteristics of a person and using this chart, you can plot his or her position on the Tone Scale and thereby know the rest, obtaining an accurate index of their *entire* personality, conduct and character. Before this book the world was convinced that cases could not improve but only deteriorate. Science of Survival presents the idea of different states of case and the brand-new idea that one can progress upward on the Tone Scale. And therein lies the basis of today's Grade Chart.

THE SCIENCE OF SURVIVAL LECTURES • Underlying the development of the Tone Scale and Chart of Human Evaluation was a monumental breakthrough: The *Theta–MEST Theory,* containing the explanation of the interaction between Life—*theta*—with the physical universe of Matter, Energy, Space and Time—*MEST.* In these lectures, delivered to students immediately following publication of the book, Ron gave the most expansive description of all that lies behind the Chart of Human Evaluation and its application in life itself. Moreover, here also is the explanation of how the ratio of *theta* and *en(turbulated)-theta* determines one's position on the Tone Scale and the means to ascend to higher states. *4 lectures.*

SELF ANALYSIS • The barriers of life are really just shadows. Learn to know yourself—not just a shadow of yourself. Containing the most complete description of consciousness, Self Analysis takes you through your past, through your potentials, your life. First, with a series of self-examinations and using a special version of the Hubbard Chart of Human Evaluation, you plot yourself on the Tone Scale. Then, applying a series of light yet powerful processes, you embark on the great adventure of self-discovery. This book further contains embracive principles that reach *any* case, from the lowest to the highest—including auditing techniques so effective they are referred to by Ron again and again through all following years of research into the highest states. In sum, this book not only moves one up the Tone Scale but can pull a person out of almost anything.

ADVANCED PROCEDURE AND AXIOMS • With new breakthroughs on the nature and anatomy of engrams—"Engrams are effective only when the individual himself determines that they will be effective"—came the discovery of the being's use of a *Service Facsimile:* a mechanism employed to explain away failures in life, but which then locks a person into detrimental patterns of behavior and further failure. In consequence came a new type of processing addressing *Thought, Emotion* and *Effort* detailed in the "Fifteen Acts" of Advanced Procedure and oriented to the rehabilitation of the preclear's *Self-determinism.* Hence, this book also contains the all-encompassing, no-excuses-allowed explanation of Full Responsibility, the key to unlocking it all. Moreover, here is the codification of *Definitions, Logics,* and *Axioms,* providing both the summation of the entire subject and direction for all future research. *See Handbook for Preclears, written as a companion self-processing manual to Advanced Procedure and Axioms.*

THOUGHT, EMOTION AND EFFORT • With the codification of the Axioms came the means to address key points on a case that could unravel all aberration. *Basic Postulates, Prime Thought, Cause and Effect* and their effect on everything from *memory* and *responsibility* to an individual's own role in empowering *engrams*—these matters are only addressed in this series. Here, too, is the most complete description of the *Service Facsimile* found anywhere—and why its resolution removes an individual's self-imposed disabilities. *21 lectures.*

HANDBOOK FOR PRECLEARS • The "Fifteen Acts" of Advanced Procedure and Axioms are paralleled by the fifteen Self-processing Acts given in Handbook for Preclears. Moreover, this book contains several essays giving the most expansive description of the *Ideal State of Man*. Discover why behavior patterns become so solidly fixed; why habits seemingly can't be broken; how decisions long ago have more power over a person than his decisions today; and why a person keeps past negative experiences in the present. It's all clearly laid out on the Chart of Attitudes—a milestone breakthrough that complements the Chart of Human Evaluation—plotting the ideal state of being and one's *attitudes* and *reactions* to life. *In self-processing, Handbook for Preclears is used in conjunction with Self Analysis.*

THE LIFE CONTINUUM • Besieged with requests for lectures on his latest breakthroughs, Ron replied with everything they wanted and more at the Second Annual Conference of Dianetic Auditors. Describing the technology that lies behind the self-processing steps of the *Handbook*—here is the *how* and *why* of it all: the discovery of *Life Continuum*—the mechanism by which an individual is compelled to carry on the life of another deceased or departed individual, generating in his own body the infirmities and mannerisms of the departed. Combined with auditor instruction on use of the Chart of Attitudes in determining how to enter every case at the proper gradient, here, too, are directions for dissemination of the Handbook and hence, the means to begin wide-scale clearing. *10 lectures.*

SCIENTOLOGY: MILESTONE ONE • Ron began the first lecture in this series with six words that would change the world forever: "This is a course in *Scientology*." From there, Ron not only described the vast scope of this, a then brand-new subject, he also detailed his discoveries on past lives. He proceeded from there to the description of the first E-Meter and its initial use in uncovering the *theta line* (the entire track of a thetan's existence), as entirely distinct from the *genetic body line* (the time track of bodies and their physical evolution), shattering the "one-life" lie and revealing the *whole track* of spiritual existence. Here, then, is the very genesis of Scientology. *22 lectures.*

THE ROUTE TO INFINITY: TECHNIQUE 80 LECTURES • As Ron explained, "Technique 80 is the *To Be or Not To Be* Technique." With that, he unveiled the crucial foundation on which ability and sanity rest: *the being's capacity to make a decision*. Here, then, is the anatomy of "maybe," the *Wavelengths of ARC,* the *Tone Scale of Decisions,* and the means to rehabilitate a being's ability *To Be*…almost *anything. 7 lectures. (Knowledge of Technique 80 is required for Technique 88 as described in Scientology: A History of Man—below.)*

SCIENTOLOGY: A HISTORY OF MAN • "A cold-blooded and factual account of your last 76 trillion years." So begins A History of Man, announcing the revolutionary *Technique 88*—revealing for the first time the truth about whole track experience and the exclusive address, in auditing, to the thetan. Here is history unraveled with the first E-Meter, delineating and describing the principal incidents on the whole track to be found in any human being: *Electronic implants, entities,* the *genetic track, between-lives incidents, how bodies evolved* and *why you got trapped in them*—they're all detailed here.

> TECHNIQUE 88: INCIDENTS ON THE TRACK BEFORE EARTH • "Technique 88 is the most hyperbolical, effervescent, dramatic, unexaggeratable, high-flown, superlative, grandiose, colossal and magnificent technique which the mind of Man could conceivably embrace. It is as big as the whole track and all the incidents on it. It's what you apply it to; it's what's been going on. It contains the riddles and secrets, the mysteries of all time. You could bannerline this technique like they do a sideshow, but nothing you could say, no adjective you could use, would adequately describe even a small segment of it. It not only batters the imagination, it makes you ashamed to imagine anything," is Ron's introduction to you in this never-before-available lecture series, expanding on all else contained in History of Man. What awaits you is the whole track itself. *15 lectures.*

SCIENTOLOGY 8 - 80 • The *first* explanation of the electronics of human thought and the energy phenomena in any being. Discover how even physical universe laws of motion are mirrored in a being, not to mention the electronics of aberration. Here is the link between theta and MEST revealing what energy *is,* and how you *create* it. It was this breakthrough that revealed the subject of a thetan's *flows* and which, in turn, is applied in *every* auditing process today. In the book's title, "8-8" stands for *Infinity–Infinity,* and "0" represents the static, *theta.* Included are the *Wavelengths of Emotion, Aesthetics, Beauty and Ugliness, Inflow and Outflow* and the *Sub-zero Tone Scale*—applicable only to the thetan.

> SOURCE OF LIFE ENERGY • Beginning with the announcement of his new book — Scientology 8-80—Ron not only unveiled his breakthroughs of theta as the Source of Life Energy, but detailed the *Methods of Research* he used to make that and every other discovery of Dianetics and Scientology: the Qs and *Logics*—methods of *thinking* applicable to any universe or thinking process. Here, then, is both *how to think* and *how to evaluate all data and knowledge,* and thus, the linchpin to a full understanding of both Scientology and life itself. *14 lectures.*

🎙 **THE COMMAND OF THETA** • While in preparation of his newest book and the Doctorate Course he was about to deliver, Ron called together auditors for a new Professional Course. As he said, "For the first time with this class we are stepping, really, beyond the scope of the word *Survival*." From that vantage point, the Command of Theta gives the technology that bridges the knowledge from 8-80 to 8-8008, and provides the first full explanation of the subject of *Cause* and a permanent shift of orientation in life from MEST to *Theta*. *10 lectures.*

SCIENTOLOGY 8 - 8008 • The complete description of the behavior and potentials of a *thetan,* and textbook for the Philadelphia Doctorate Course and The Factors: Admiration and the Renaissance of Beingness lectures. As Ron said, the book's title serves to fix in the mind of the individual a route by which he can rehabilitate himself, his abilities, his ethics and his goals—the attainment of *infinity* (8) by the reduction of the apparent *infinity* (8) of the MEST universe to *zero* (0) and the increase of the apparent *zero* (0) of one's own universe to *infinity* (8). Condensed herein are more than 80,000 hours of investigation, with a summarization and amplification of every breakthrough to date—and the full significance of those discoveries form the new vantage point of *Operating Thetan.*

🎙 **THE PHILADELPHIA DOCTORATE COURSE LECTURES** • This renowned series stands as the largest single body of work on the anatomy, behavior and potentials of the spirit of Man ever assembled, providing the very fundamentals which underlie the route to Operating Thetan. Here it is in complete detail—the thetan's relationship to the *creation, maintenance* and *destruction of universes.* In just those terms, here is the *anatomy* of matter, energy, space and time, and *postulating* universes into existence. Here, too, is the thetan's fall from whole track abilities and the *universal laws* by which they are restored. In short, here is Ron's codification of the upper echelon of theta beingness and behavior. Lecture after lecture fully expands every concept of the course text, Scientology 8-8008, providing the total scope of *you* in native state. *76 lectures and accompanying reproductions of the original 54 LRH hand-drawn lecture charts.*

🎙 **THE FACTORS: ADMIRATION AND THE RENAISSANCE OF BEINGNESS** • With the *potentials* of a thetan fully established came a look outward resulting in Ron's monumental discovery of a *universal solvent* and the basic laws of the theta *universe*—laws quite literally senior to anything: *The Factors: Summation of the Considerations of the Human Spirit and Material Universe.* So dramatic were these breakthroughs, Ron expanded the book Scientology 8-8008, both clarifying previous discoveries and adding chapter after chapter which, studied with these lectures, provide a postgraduate level to the Doctorate Course. Here then are lectures containing the knowledge of *universal truth* unlocking the riddle of creation itself. *18 lectures.*

THE CREATION OF HUMAN ABILITY—*A HANDBOOK FOR SCIENTOLOGISTS* • On the heels of his discoveries of Operating Thetan came a year of intensive research, exploring the realm of a *thetan exterior.* Through auditing and instruction, including 450 lectures in this same twelve-month span, Ron codified the entire subject of Scientology. And it's all contained in this handbook, from a *Summary of Scientology* to its basic *Axioms* and *Codes.* Moreover, here is *Intensive Procedure,* containing the famed Exteriorization Processes of *Route 1* and *Route 2*—processes drawn right from the Axioms. Each one is described in detail—*how* the process is used, *why* it works, the axiomatic technology that underlies its use, and the complete explanation of how a being can break the *false agreements* and *self-created barriers* that enslave him to the physical universe. In short, this book contains the ultimate summary of thetan exterior OT ability and its permanent accomplishment.

PHOENIX LECTURES: FREEING THE HUMAN SPIRIT • Here is the panoramic view of Scientology complete. Having codified the subject of Scientology in Creation of Human Ability, Ron then delivered a series of half-hour lectures to specifically accompany a full study of the book. From the *essentials* that underlie the technology—*The Axioms, Conditions of Existence* and *Considerations and Mechanics,* to the processes of *Intensive Procedure,* including twelve lectures describing one-by-one the thetan exterior processes of *Route 1*—it's all covered in full, providing a conceptual understanding of the *science of knowledge* and *native state OT ability.* Here then are the bedrock principles upon which everything in Scientology rests, including the embracive statement of the religion and its heritage—*Scientology, Its General Background.* Hence, this is the watershed lecture series on Scientology itself, and the axiomatic foundation for all future research. *42 lectures.*

DIANETICS 55!—*THE COMPLETE MANUAL OF HUMAN COMMUNICATION* • With all breakthroughs to date, a single factor had been isolated as crucial to success in every type of auditing. As LRH said, "Communication is so thoroughly important today in Dianetics and Scientology (as it always has been on the whole track) that it could be said if you were to get a preclear into communication, you would get him well." And this book delineates the *exact,* but previously unknown, anatomy and formulas for *perfect* communication. The magic of the communication cycle is *the* fundamental of auditing and the primary reason auditing works. The breakthroughs here opened new vistas of application—discoveries of such magnitude, LRH called Dianetics 55! the *Second Book* of Dianetics.

THE UNIFICATION CONGRESS: COMMUNICATION! FREEDOM & ABILITY • The historic Congress announcing the reunification of the subjects of Dianetics and Scientology with the release of *Dianetics 55!* Until now, each had operated in their own sphere: Dianetics addressed Man *as Man*—the first four dynamics, while Scientology addressed *life itself*—the Fifth to Eighth Dynamics. The formula which would serve as the foundation for all future development was contained in a single word: *Communication.* It was a paramount breakthrough Ron would later call, "the great discovery of Dianetics and Scientology." Here, then, are the lectures, as it happened. *16 lectures and accompanying reproductions of the original LRH hand-drawn lecture charts.*

SCIENTOLOGY: THE FUNDAMENTALS OF THOUGHT—*THE BASIC BOOK OF THE THEORY AND PRACTICE OF SCIENTOLOGY FOR BEGINNERS* • Designated by Ron as the *Book One of Scientology*. After having fully unified and codified the subjects of Dianetics and Scientology came the refinement of their *fundamentals*. Originally published as a résumé of Scientology for use in translations into non-English tongues, this book is of inestimable value to both the beginner and advanced student of the mind, spirit and life. Equipped with this book alone, one can begin a practice and perform seeming miracle changes in the states of well-being, ability and intelligence of people. Contained within are the *Conditions of Existence, Eight Dynamics, ARC Triangle, Parts of Man,* the full analysis of *Life as a Game,* and more, including exact processes for individual application of these principles in processing. Here, then, in one book, is the starting point for bringing Scientology to people everywhere.

HUBBARD PROFESSIONAL COURSE LECTURES • While Fundamentals of Thought stands as an introduction to the subject for beginners, it also contains a distillation of fundamentals for every Scientologist. Here are the in-depth descriptions of those fundamentals, each lecture one-half hour in length and providing, one-by-one, a complete mastery of a single Scientology breakthrough—*Axioms 1–10; The Anatomy of Control; Handling of Problems; Start, Change and Stop; Confusion and Stable Data; Exteriorization; Valences* and more—the *why* behind them, *how* they came to be and their mechanics. And it's all brought together with the *Code of a Scientologist,* point by point, and its use in actually creating a new civilization. In short, here are the LRH lectures that make a *Professional Scientologist*—one who can apply the subject to every aspect of life. *21 lectures.*

Additional Books Containing Scientology Essentials

Work

The Problems of Work—*Scientology Applied to the Workaday World* • Having codified the entire subject of Scientology, Ron immediately set out to provide the *beginning* manual for its application by anyone. As he described it: life is composed of seven-tenths work, one-tenth familial, one-tenth political and one-tenth relaxation. Here, then, is Scientology applied to that seven-tenths of existence including the answers to *Exhaustion* and the *Secret of Efficiency.* Here, too, is the analysis of life itself—a game composed of exact rules. Know them and you succeed. Problems of Work contains technology no one can live without, and that can immediately be applied by both the Scientologist and those new to the subject.

Life Principles

Scientology: A New Slant on Life • Scientology essentials for every aspect of life. Basic answers that put you in charge of your existence, truths to consult again and again: *Is It Possible to Be Happy?, Two Rules for Happy Living, Personal Integrity, The Anti-Social Personality* and many more. In every part of this book you will find Scientology truths that describe conditions in your life and furnish *exact* ways to improve them. Scientology: A New Slant on Life contains essential knowledge for every Scientologist and a perfect introduction for anyone new to the subject.

Axioms, Codes and Scales

Scientology 0 - 8: The Book of Basics • The companion to *all* Ron's books, lectures and materials. This is *the* Book of Basics, containing indispensable data you will refer to constantly: the *Axioms of Dianetics and Scientology; The Factors;* a full compilation of all *Scales*—more than 100 in all; listings of the *Perceptics* and *Awareness Levels;* all *Codes* and *Creeds* and much more. The senior laws of existence are condensed into this single volume, distilled from more than 15,000 pages of writings, 3,000 lectures and scores of books.

SCIENTOLOGY ETHICS:
TECHNOLOGY OF OPTIMUM SURVIVAL

INTRODUCTION TO SCIENTOLOGY ETHICS • A new hope for Man arises with the first workable technology of ethics—technology to help an individual pull himself out of the downward skid of life and to a higher plateau of survival. This is the comprehensive handbook providing the crucial fundamentals: *Basics of Ethics & Justice; Honesty; Conditions of Existence; Condition Formulas* from Confusion to Power; the *Basics of Suppression* and its handling; as well as *Justice Procedures* and their use in Scientology Churches. Here, then, is the technology to overcome any barriers in life and in one's personal journey up the Bridge to Total Freedom.

PURIFICATION

CLEAR BODY, CLEAR MIND—*THE EFFECTIVE PURIFICATION PROGRAM* • We live in a biochemical world, and this book is the solution. While investigating the harmful effects that earlier drug use had on preclears' cases, Ron made the major discovery that many street drugs, particularly LSD, remained in a person's body long after ingested. Residues of the drug, he noted, could have serious and lasting effects, including triggering further "trips." Additional research revealed that a wide range of substances—medical drugs, alcohol, pollutants, household chemicals and even food preservatives—could also lodge in the body's tissues. Through research on thousands of cases, he developed the *Purification Program* to eliminate their destructive effects. Clear Body, Clear Mind details every aspect of the all-natural regimen that can free one from the harmful effects of drugs and other toxins, opening the way for spiritual progress.

Reference Handbooks

WHAT IS SCIENTOLOGY?

The complete and essential encyclopedic reference on the subject and practice of Scientology. Organized for use, this book contains the pertinent data on every aspect of the subject:

• The life of L. Ron Hubbard and his path of discovery

• The Spiritual Heritage of the religion

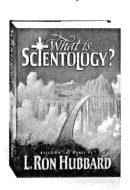

• A full description of Dianetics and Scientology

• Auditing—what it is and how it works

• Courses—what they contain and how they are structured

• The Grade Chart of Services and how one ascends to higher states

• The Scientology Ethics and Justice System

• The Organizational Structure of the Church

• A complete description of the many Social Betterment programs supported by the Church, including: Drug Rehabilitation, Criminal Reform, Literacy and Education and the instilling of real values for morality

Over 1,000 pages in length, with more than 500 photographs and illustrations, this text further includes Creeds, Codes, a full listing of all books and materials as well as a Catechism with answers to virtually any question regarding the subject.

You Ask and This Book Answers.

THE SCIENTOLOGY HANDBOOK

Scientology fundamentals for daily use in every part of life. Encompassing 19 separate bodies of technology, here is the most comprehensive manual on the basics of life ever published. Each chapter contains key principles and technology for your continual use:

• Study Technology

• The Dynamics of Existence

• The Components of Understanding— Affinity, Reality and Communication

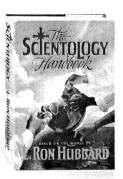

• The Tone Scale

• Communication and its Formulas

• Assists for Illnesses and Injuries

• How to Resolve Conflicts

• Integrity and Honesty

• Ethics and Condition Formulas

• Answers to Suppression and a Dangerous Environment

• Marriage

• Children

• Tools for the Workplace

More than 700 photographs and illustrations make it easy for you to learn the procedures and apply them at once. This book is truly the indispensable handbook for every Scientologist.

The Technology to Build a Better World.

About L. Ron Hubbard

"To really know life," L. Ron Hubbard wrote, "you've got to be part of life. You must get down and look, you must get into the nooks and crannies of existence. You have to rub elbows with all kinds and types of men before you can finally establish what he is."

Through his long and extraordinary journey to the founding of Dianetics and Scientology, Ron did just that. From his adventurous youth in a rough and tumble American West to his far-flung trek across a still mysterious Asia; from his two-decade search for the very essence of life to the triumph of Dianetics and Scientology—such are the stories recounted in the L. Ron Hubbard Biographical Publications.

Presenting the photographic overview of Ron's greater journey is *L. Ron Hubbard: Images of a Lifetime.* Drawn from his own archival collection, this is Ron's life as he himself saw it.

While for the many aspects of that rich and varied life, stands the Ron Series. Each issue focuses on a specific LRH profession: *Auditor, Humanitarian, Philosopher, Artist, Poet, Music Maker, Photographer* and many more including his published articles on *Freedom* and his personal *Letters & Journals.* Here is the life of a man who lived at least twenty lives in the space of one.

FOR FURTHER INFORMATION VISIT
www.lronhubbard.org

GUIDE TO THE MATERIALS

YOU'RE ON AN ADVENTURE!
HERE'S THE MAP.

- All books
- All lectures
- All reference books

All of it laid out in chronological sequence with descriptions of what each contains.

Your journey to a full understanding of Dianetics and Scientology is the greatest adventure of all. But you need a map that shows you where you are and where you are going.

That map is the Materials Guide Chart. It shows all Ron's books and lectures with a full description of their content and subject matter so you can find exactly what *you* are looking for and precisely what *you* need.

Since each book and lecture is laid out in chronological sequence, you can see *how* the subjects of Dianetics and Scientology were developed. And what that means is by simply studying this chart you are in for cognition after cognition!

New editions of all books include extensive glossaries, containing definitions for every technical term. And as a result of a monumental restoration program, the entire library of Ron's lectures are being made available on compact disc, with complete transcripts, glossaries, lecture graphs, diagrams and issues he refers to in the lectures. As a result, you get *all* the data, and can learn with ease, gaining a full *conceptual* understanding.

And what that adds up to is a new Golden Age of Knowledge every Dianeticist and Scientologist has dreamed of.

To obtain your FREE Materials Guide Chart and Catalog, or to order L. Ron Hubbard's books and lectures, contact:

WESTERN HEMISPHERE:

**Bridge
Publications, Inc.**
4751 Fountain Avenue
Los Angeles, CA 90029 USA
www.bridgepub.com
Phone: 1-800-722-1733
Fax: 1-323-953-3328

EASTERN HEMISPHERE:

**New Era Publications
International ApS**
Store Kongensgade 53
1264 Copenhagen K, Denmark
www.newerapublications.com
Phone: (45) 33 73 66 66
Fax: (45) 33 73 66 33

Books and lectures are also available direct from Churches of Scientology.
See Addresses.

Addresses

Dianetics is a forerunner and substudy of Scientology, the fastest-growing religion in the world today. Centers and Churches exist in cities throughout the world, and new ones are continually forming.

Dianetics Centers offer introductory services and can help you begin your journey, or get you started on the adventure of Dianetics auditing. To obtain more information or to locate the Dianetics Center nearest you, visit the Dianetics website:

www.dianetics.org
e-mail: info@dianetics.org
or
Phone: 1-800-367-8788
(for US and Canada)

Every Church of Scientology contains a Dianetics Center, offering both introductory services as well as formalized training in the subject. They can also provide further information about Mr. Hubbard's later discoveries on the subject of Scientology. For more information, visit:

www.scientology.org
e-mail: info@scientology.org
or
Phone: 1-800-334-LIFE
(for US and Canada)

You can also write to any one of the Continental Organizations, listed on the following page, who can direct you to one of the thousands of Centers and Churches world over.

L. Ron Hubbard's books and lectures may be obtained from any of these addresses or direct from the publishers on the previous page.

CONTINENTAL ORGANIZATIONS:

UNITED STATES

CONTINENTAL LIAISON OFFICE
WESTERN UNITED STATES
1308 L. Ron Hubbard Way
Los Angeles, California 90027 USA

CONTINENTAL LIAISON OFFICE
EASTERN UNITED STATES
349 W. 48th Street
New York, New York 10036 USA

CANADA

CONTINENTAL LIAISON OFFICE
CANADA
696 Yonge Street, 2nd Floor
Toronto, Ontario
Canada M4Y 2A7

LATIN AMERICA

CONTINENTAL LIAISON OFFICE
LATIN AMERICA
Federacion Mexicana de Dianetica
Calle Puebla #31
Colonia Roma, Mexico D.F.
C.P. 06700, Mexico

UNITED KINGDOM

CONTINENTAL LIAISON OFFICE
UNITED KINGDOM
Saint Hill Manor
East Grinstead, West Sussex
England, RH19 4JY

AFRICA

CONTINENTAL LIAISON OFFICE AFRICA
5 Cynthia Street
Kensington
Johannesburg 2094, South Africa

AUSTRALIA, NEW ZEALAND & OCEANIA
CONTINENTAL LIAISON OFFICE ANZO
16 Dorahy Street
Dundas, New South Wales 2117
Australia

Liaison Office of Taiwan
1st, No. 231, Cisian 2nd Road
Kaoshiung City
Taiwan, ROC

EUROPE
CONTINENTAL LIAISON OFFICE EUROPE
Store Kongensgade 55
1264 Copenhagen K, Denmark

**Liaison Office of Commonwealth
of Independent States**
Management Center of Dianetics
and Scientology Dissemination
Pervomajskaya Street, House 1A
Korpus Grazhdanskoy Oboroni
Losino-Petrovsky Town
141150 Moscow, Russia

Liaison Office of Central Europe
1082 Leonardo da Vinci u. 8-14
Budapest, Hungary

Liaison Office of Iberia
C/Miguel Menendez Boneta, 18
28460 – Los Molinos
Madrid, Spain

Liaison Office of Italy
Via Cadorna, 61
20090 Vimodrone
Milan, Italy

Become a Member
OF THE INTERNATIONAL ASSOCIATION OF SCIENTOLOGISTS

The International Association of Scientologists is the membership organization of all Scientologists united in the most vital crusade on Earth.

A free Six-Month Introductory Membership is extended to anyone who has not held a membership with the Association before.

As a member, you are eligible for discounts on Scientology materials offered only to IAS Members. You also receive the Association magazine, *IMPACT,* issued six times a year, full of Scientology news from around the world.

The purpose of the IAS is:

"To unite, advance, support and protect Scientology and Scientologists in all parts of the world so as to achieve the Aims of Scientology as originated by L. Ron Hubbard."

Join the strongest force for positive change on the planet today, opening the lives of millions to the greater truth embodied in Scientology.

JOIN THE INTERNATIONAL ASSOCIATION OF SCIENTOLOGISTS.

To apply for membership,
write to the International
Association of Scientologists
c/o Saint Hill Manor, East Grinstead
West Sussex, England, RH19 4JY

www.iasmembership.org

Editor's Glossary

OF WORDS, TERMS & PHRASES

Words often have several meanings. The definitions used here only give the meaning that the word has as it is used in this book. Dianetics terms appear in bold type. Beside each definition you will find the page on which it first appears, so you can refer back to the text if you wish.

This glossary is not meant to take the place of standard language or Dianetics and Scientology dictionaries, which should be referred to for any words, terms or phrases that do not appear below.

The chapter LRH Glossary should be read, in full, for a proper grounding in the nomenclature of this subject. Definitions from that chapter are, however, included below for ease of reference and are noted where they occur.

—The Editors

AA: AN ATTEMPTED ABORTION CASE. (From *LRH Glossary.*)

abbreviate: to reduce something; make less. Page 9.

aberrated: affected by aberration. Page 18.

aberration(s): comes from Latin *aberrare,* to wander from; *ab,* away, *errare,* to wander. Hence, a departure from rational thought or behavior. In Dianetics it further means the aberree's reaction to and difficulties with his current environment. See rest of text for use of and explanation of its cause and remedy. Page 7.

ABERREE: AN ABERRATED INDIVIDUAL, SANE OR INSANE, CONTAINING UNRELIEVED ENGRAMS. (From *LRH Glossary.*) Page 36.

ABNORMAL DIANETICS: THAT BRANCH OF DIANETICS WHICH INCLUDES THE AXIOMS AND PROCESSES OF THE SCIENCE WHICH TREATS THE ABERRATED MIND, INCLUDING ALL TECHNIQUES NECESSARY TO THE ALLEVIATION OR CURE OF SUCH ABERRATIONS AND ESTABLISHING A TONE 4 IN THE INDIVIDUAL. IT DOES NOT EMBRACE THE STUDY OF THOSE WHO ARE INSANE THROUGH ANATOMICAL DEFICIENCIES OR THROUGH INJURY. THESE ARE A SUBJECT FOR RESEARCH UNDER DYNAMIC DIANETICS. (From *LRH Glossary.*) Page vii.

abyss: a vast or bottomless opening, void space, etc., thought of as leading to or containing something immensely harmful, destructive, etc. Page 13.

accord, of their own: voluntarily or spontaneously; done without any prompting. Page 142.

accounted: looked upon, rated, regarded or classified as. Page 157.

account for: give satisfactory reason for, explain. Page 26.

account, taken into: considered along with other factors before observing something, reaching a decision or taking action. Page 97.

acute: brief or having a short course as opposed to chronic (long-lasting, said of a condition that lasts over a long period). Page 150.

additive: involving or produced by addition or by the addition of something. Page 171.

adhere: follow or maintain steadily and consistently. Page 103.

admit: allow the possibility of. Page 7.

affinity: agreement; a natural friendliness, liking for or attraction to a person, thing, idea, etc. Page 13.

aggravated: annoyed; irritated; exasperated. Page 81.

aggregate: 1. gather into one. Page 25.
2. sum, mass or assemblage of particulars; a total or gross amount. Page 39.

aggregation (colonial): a group of organisms formed together into a connected structure and living or growing in close association with each other. *Colonial* in this sense means pertaining to or of a group or mass of individual animals or plants, of the same kind, living or growing in close association. *Aggregation* is used in its biological sense, the act or process of organisms coming together to form a group. Page 9.

allay(ed): subdue or reduce in intensity or severity. Page 100.

allergies: unusual sensitivity to normally harmless substances (such as dust, pollen, foods, etc.) that when breathed in, swallowed or brought into contact with the skin, provoke a strong reaction from the person's body. Page 1.

alleviate: to lighten or lessen the pain, severity, etc., of something; relieve. Page 139.

alliance: a union or association formed for mutual benefit. Also, a relationship based on an affinity. Page 171.

allocated: set apart for a specific purpose. Page 17.

amentia, physiological: a condition or instance characterized by lack of intellectual development or severe mental retardation from a birth defect or from damage to the brain in early childhood. *Physiological* means of or pertaining to the functions and activities of living organisms and their parts, including all physical and chemical processes. Page 54.

amnesia-tranced: in an *amnesia trance,* a deep trance of a person as if asleep, making him susceptible to commands. *Amnesia* in this sense refers to the fact that the person cannot remember what took place during the deep trance state. Page 43.

amount to: to be essentially equal to a particular thing in effect, outcome or value. Page 82.

amplified: developed or expanded as by additional information, details, examples or the like. Page viii.

analogically: like an analogy. *See* **analogy.** Page 40.

analogy: a comparison between two things that are similar in some respects, often used to help explain something or make it easier to understand. Page 17.

analytical: of *analysis,* the action of rationally looking at or computing data such as by separating it into parts to study or examine, draw conclusions or solve problems. Page viii.

ANALYTICAL MIND: THE RESIDENCE OF CONSCIOUSNESS IN THE INDIVIDUAL AND THE SEAT OF HIS DYNAMICS AND BASIC PERSONALITY. THIS IS AN ANALOGICAL TERM. THE ANALYTICAL MIND CAN BE SUBDIVIDED. (From *LRH Glossary.*) Page viii.

analyzer: 1. a thing which *analyzes,* rationally looks at or computes data such as separating it into parts to study or examine, draw conclusions or solve problems. Page 11.

2. in Dianetics, the analyzer is the analytical mind. The analyzer is fully described in Chapter Thirteen, The Analyzer. Page 19.

anatomy (human): a person's body. Page 47.

ancestor(s): one from whom a person is descended, especially one who existed in the distant past. Page 10.

anguish: extreme distress, suffering or pain. Page 45.

antipathetic: opposed or contrary. Page 27.

antipathies: feelings of disgust toward something, usually together with an intense desire to avoid or turn from it. Page 70.

apathy: lack of interest in anything or the absence of any wish to do anything. Page 59.

appalled: filled or overcome with shock or horror. Page 159.

appended: attached to or joined on. Page 105.

appreciation(s): 1. expressions of gratitude, recognition, etc. Page 9. **2.** clear perception or recognition of the value or significance of something. Page 114.

appreciator: something that makes or forms an estimate, as of worth, quality or amount. Page 68.

apprised: aware or informed. Page 68.

approximation(s): 1. something that is similar in quantity, quality or degree to something else. An approximation of the reactive mind would be a person, object, sound or the like in the environment that is similar to a recording in the reactive mind. Page 20. **2.** a demonstration or example of something (such as an engram) that is similar to the actual thing in quality, nature or degree. Page 43.

arbitrary: something derived from mere opinion or preference; something unreasonable or unsupported. Page 59.

arduous: requiring great exertion, energy or strong effort. Page 46.

arrest: stop or slow someone down. Page 54.

arthritis: inflammation of the joints, causing pain, swelling and stiffness. Page 1.

articulate: clearly express in words. Page 167.

artistry: creative ability and skill. Page 36.

as in: as regards, with respect or reference to. Page 67.

as long as: under the condition that; provided that. Page 49.

aspect(s): 1. nature; quality; character. Page 17.

2. the state, condition or manner in which a person or object appears to the eye; the outward look of someone or something. Page 56.

assignation: the act of assigning, specifying or selecting; fixing exactly. Page 59.

assist engram: an engram with "complimentary" content which can bring about a manic state (that of abnormal excitability, exaggerated feelings of well-being, etc.). The assist engram is further described in Chapter Sixteen, Dramatization. Page 150.

association: the connection or relation of ideas, feelings, sensations; correlation of the elements of perception, reasoning or the like. Page 54.

Associative Restimulator: a perceptic in the environment which is confused with an actual restimulator. (From *LRH Glossary*.)

as such: as the word just referenced is usually understood; as being what the name or description implies; in that capacity, as in *"These are in essence unsolved problems. As such, they contain their own solutions."* Page 67.

assume(d): 1. to accept something as existing or being true without definite proof; suppose, as in *"If it vanishes without attaining the laughter of Tone 4, it can be assumed that the individual's basic engram has not been erased."* Page 60.

2. take upon oneself, as a responsibility, obligation, etc., as in *"The auditor should therefore, when he undertakes a case, be prepared to assume the family of his preclear."* Page 108.

3. take on a particular quality, character, state or the like, as in *"Actually, it is not even of interest to the auditor how many personalities the 'awake' aberrated individual has assumed or can manifest."* Page 128.

asthma: a generally chronic disorder characterized by wheezing, coughing, difficulty in breathing and a suffocating feeling. Page 1.

astigmatism: a visual defect caused by the unequal curving of the surface of the eye. It prevents light rays from coming to a focus, thus producing blurred vision. Page 1.

at all costs: whatever effort is needed; in spite of all losses; whatever happens. Page 81.

at hand: within reach; nearby; ready for use. Page 157.

at least: 1. used to limit or make what has just been stated less definite, as in *"Man is the most successful organism currently in existence, at least on this planet."* Page 10.

2. not less than, as in *"Anyone who has been born, then, possesses at least one engram."* Page 48.

at length: after some time; eventually. Page 104.

attain(ment): arrive at or obtain something. Page 13.

attendant(ly): (in a manner that is) accompanying, connecting with or immediately following as a consequence. Page 27.

attuned: adjusted or accustomed so as to become receptive or responsive. Page 19.

at will: just as or when one wishes. Page 88.

at work: in operation; having an effect on something. Page 108.

audio-syllabic: the spoken word. From *audio-,* sound within the range of human hearing, and *syllable,* a word or part of a word pronounced with a single, uninterrupted sounding of the voice. Page 39.

auditing: the application of Dianetics procedures to someone by a trained auditor. Page viii.

auditor: the term *auditor* is used in Dianetics to designate someone skilled in the practice of Dianetic therapy. To *audit* is to both listen and compute. Page 28.

"automatic determinism," the doctrine of: the belief that action, thought, imagination, creativity, etc., is caused by stimulus-response; that is, a certain stimulus (something that rouses a person or thing to activity or that produces a reaction in the body) automatically giving a certain response. This doctrine was exemplified by Ivan Petrovich Pavlov (1849–1936), Russian physiologist, noted for his dog experiments. Pavlov presented food (stimulus) to a dog, while he sounded a bell (also a stimulus). After repeating this procedure several times, the dog (in anticipation) would salivate at the sound of the bell, whether or not food was presented. Pavlov concluded that all acquired habits, even the higher mental activity of Man, depended on such stimulus-response. Page 130.

axioms: statements of natural laws on the order of those of the physical sciences. Page 1.

badger: harass or urge persistently, especially in a manner likely or designed to annoy. Page 81.

banked: entered or retained in a *bank,* a storage place for information, as in computers where data is stored in computer memory called, collectively, a bank. Used to describe a storage of memory information in the mind. Page 156.

base: low in scale or rank. Hence, having or showing little or no decency and honor, lacking in higher values. Page 132.

basic engram: *basic* here refers to the starting point of something. The basic engram is the first or earliest engram an individual has received, as in *"The discovery of the* basic engram *is the first problem of the auditor."* Page 49.

basic personality: the individual himself. Page viii.

beholds: holds in view; looks at or observes. Page 106.

birthright: a right or the rights that a person has because of being born such as in a certain group, family, nation, etc. Page 110.

blast: blow away or expel something with force or violence, in reference to the action of *shock treatment,* any of various methods of supposedly treating certain mental disorders by use of drugs, electric current, etc., to bring about convulsion (uncontrollable shaking of the body) to overcome emotional difficulty. Page 132.

blunt: 1. plain-spoken, honest or frank. Page 110.

   2. insensitive; stupid. Page 116.

bounce: move quickly (into play); spring or jump (forward). Page 148.

bracket: a category of things that fall between specified limits. Page 59.

break(s)(ing): 1. divides into smaller units or components, as in *"Each one of the four dynamics breaks further into purposes which are specific and complex."* Page 26.

   2. failing to conform to or acting contrary to (one's word, a promise, etc.), as in *"The auditor must be* trustworthy, *never betraying or capriciously denying a preclear and, above all, never breaking his word to the preclear."* Page 81.

3. weaken or crush in strength, spirit, etc.; discourage mentally or spiritually. Page 94.

4. to put an end to; overcome; stop, as in *"The entire intent and technique of Dianetics is to break the partial or complete suppression of the analytical mind."* Page 118.

BREAK ENGRAM: THE ENGRAM LOCK AFTER THE RECEIPT OF WHICH THE INDIVIDUAL EXPERIENCED A LOWERING OF GENERAL TONE TO 2.5 OR LESS AND BECAME THEREFORE UNABLE TO COPE WITH HIS ENVIRONMENT. (From *LRH Glossary*.)

break point: the condition or level where an individual enters the region of insanity on the Tone Scale, between 2.0 and 2.5, and below. (Literally, a break point is the point or degree of stress at which a particular material becomes damaged so that it separates into pieces.) Page 66.

brevity: the quality of being brief or concise or expressing much in a few words. Page 114.

bring forth: produce; cause something to happen or exist. Page 116.

broken: weakened or crushed in strength, spirit, etc.; discouraged mentally or spiritually. Page 49.

bursitis: inflammation of a fluid-filled sac (bursa) of the body, particularly at the elbow, knee or shoulder joint. Page 1.

but: only; just; not more than. Page 39.

buttonhooks: instruments which were used for pulling buttons through buttonholes on boots, gloves, etc., usually a tiny hook at the end of a shaft which is affixed to a handle. Page 159.

bypass: avoid (something) by using an alternative channel, passage or route. Page 20.

bypass circuit: a reference to a path for directing part or all of an electric current around one or more elements of a circuit. Used to describe something similar in the mind. Page 66.

by reason of: because of, due to. Page 66.

by the way: used to introduce something that is not strictly part of the subject at hand; in passing as a side topic. Page 96.

cable, slap of the: a reference to the sound made by the belts (cables) of a dentist's rotating drill. The drill was connected to a motor through a series of belts that sometimes made a slapping sound against the metal arm to which they were affixed. Page 44.

called upon: required, demanded or needed (as by circumstances, etc.). Page 54.

capriciously: characterized by unpredictable changes or impulses rather than by judgment or settled purpose. Page 81.

careless: having no care, concern or interest; not caring. Page 70.

carelessness: the state in which a person is free from *care,* a feeling of worry or anxiety about something. Page 59.

case: a general term for a person being helped or audited, as in *"Birth remained inactive in the above case as a floater until the moment of reduced analytical power at the age of seven when a birth phrase was repeated."* Page 46.

case(s): 1. an instance of something; an occurrence; an example, as in *"Words are sounds in syllabic form, delivered with a definite timbre, pitch and volume or sight recognition in each case."* Page 39.
2. the circumstances or particular problem of a person who requires or receives assistance, as in *"As he works with any individual, sane or insane, he must continually employ in the bulk of his computation on the case the equation of engramic thinking."* Page 66.
3. the actual state of things, as in *"This is very far from the case with the auditor who handles continually the vital and highly charged data which* cause *physical and mental aberrations."* Page 166.

cast: literally, the actors or players in a performance. Hence, those involved in some incident, event, occurrence or the like, and by extension as used here, in the reactive mind. Page 95.

cathode ray tube: a device used in electronic equipment to display pictures, like that used in a television set. A special gun and system for focusing and changing angle (*"scanning mechanism"*) are located at one end of a glass tube. The gun sends off a beam of minute negatively charged particles (electrons) to a screen coated with a chemical that produces a fluorescent glow where the electrons strike. As the beam rapidly scans or sweeps across the entire screen with varying intensity, images are formed on the screen. (*Cathode* refers to the section of the tube that emits negatively charged particles and *cathode ray,* the name given to these energy flows when they were discovered in the 1870s.) Page 96.

causation: the power, influence or source by which something comes into existence, an action takes place or by which an effect is created. Page 18.

cell(s): the smallest structural unit of an organism that is capable of independent functioning. All plants and animals are made up of one or more cells. For instance, the human body has more than 10 trillion cells. Page 8.

cellular: having to do with a cell. Page 10.

cellular conservatism: the tendency of cells to preserve their existing and established traits and characteristics and to pass these on to the next generation of cells. Page 10.

central control system: central nervous system, consisting of a brain and spinal cord. It functions as the control center of the nervous system by receiving information from the senses and sending impulses to muscles and other parts of the body that trigger the required actions. Page 9.

cessation: a stopping of some action, activity or the like. Page 19.

chain: a series of things connected or following in succession, such as a chain of events, etc. *See* **ENGRAM CHAIN**. Page 19.

charge: 1. a quantity of energy, such as electricity, which can be stored or can flow from one point to another. Page 40.
2. suffusion (gradual spreading through or over), as with emotion, such as hopelessness. Page 65.

charged: given as a responsibility or duty; entrusted with a task, as in *"It* [the analytical mind] *is charged with the command of the dynamics."* Page 115.

charge, have (in): under one's care, control and responsibility. Page 44.

charges: persons or things that are entrusted to someone's care. Page 115.

charlatan: one who pretends to have special knowledge or skill; a fake. Page 86.

choice, power of: the ability or capacity to determine or decide something (such as a course of action). Page 113.

Christlike: resembling the characteristics representative of Jesus Christ as honesty, integrity, truth, courage, patience, compassion, etc. Page 81.

chronic: long-lasting or happening continually, as of an illness, medical or other condition. Page 49.

chronically: in a manner that lasts a long time or recurs often. Page 20.

circuit: in electricity, a complete route traveled by an electric current and which carries out a specific action, such as supplying electricity to a light bulb. In Dianetics it is used as an analogy to the mind with the same meaning. Page 40.

circuit, out of: literally, disconnected. From an electrical term meaning switched off and not part of a circuit supplying electrical power. A *circuit* is a complete route traveled by an electric current and which carries out a specific action, such as supplying electricity to a light bulb. Page 22.

circumvent: avoid or get around (an obstacle or something in the way). Page 171.

clairvoyance: the apparent power of perceiving things or events in the future or beyond normal sensory content. Page 8.

Clear: an individual who has been cleared of all engrams and engram chains and who has achieved a general Tone 4. (From *LRH Glossary*.) Page 33.

clear: free or get rid of; delete (engrams, locks, chains, etc.) from the reactive mind. Page 98.

cleared: (of the reactive mind) had engrams, locks, chains, etc., deleted. *See also* **clearing**. Page 54.

clearing: 1. the action of freeing or getting rid of. Hence, the *clearing of engrams* is the action of freeing the painful and damaging content of engrams received during unconsciousness. The term *clear* comes from computer parlance where a computer or calculator is cleared to make ready for the calculating of new problems. Page 105.

2. the action of deleting (clearing) from the reactive mind all physically painful experiences that have resulted in the aberration of the analytical mind. Page 108.

cleavage: a splitting or dividing. Page 174.

clinical(ly): purely scientifically. Also, based on actual observation of individuals rather than theory. Page 34.

codified: arranged in an organized system or orderly classification. Page 88.

colonial aggregation: a group of organisms formed together into a connected structure and living or growing in close association with each other. *Colonial* in this sense means pertaining to or of a group or mass of individual animals or plants, of the same kind, living or growing in close association. *Aggregation* is used in its biological sense, the act or process of organisms coming together to form a group. Page 9.

colony: a group or mass of individual animals or plants, of the same kind, living or growing in close association. Page 8.

commencement: the beginning of something. Page 95.

common denominator, lowest: the most fundamental factor held in common by a number of people or things. Page 8.

company: a military unit consisting of approximately sixty to one hundred and ninety troops. Page 27.

comparative energies: a reference to the fact that if one entity or thing has more energy in comparison to another, it will be stronger, more powerful, of greater intensity, etc., than that of the lesser energy. *Energy* is used here in the physics sense, the ability something has to work or move. Page 117.

compatible: consistent or in keeping with something else. Page 44.

compel: force or drive, especially into a course of action. Page 150.

compensation: payment given as an equivalent, or to make amends for a loss, damage, unemployment due to injury, etc. A *lump sum disability compensation* would be a one-time payment to compensate someone who was injured and unable to perform duty, such as from an injury received in wartime. Page 1.

complexion: general appearance or nature; character; aspect. Page 56.

complication(s): a confused or complex state of affairs caused by many interrelated factors. Page 70.

composite: something made up of separate parts or elements. Page 19.

compound(s): 1. a substance containing two or more elements (substances that themselves cannot be broken down into simpler substances) in exact proportions. A compound can be made up of many elements and usually has properties unlike those of the elements it is made up of. Compounds may be solids, liquids or gases. Page 25.
2. consisting in its nature of a combination of various parts; complex; involving the combination of various actions, processes, ideas, etc. Page 118.

compulsion(s): an irresistible impulse that is irrational or contrary to one's own will. A *compulsion* may be conceived to be an engramic command that the organism *must* do something. Page 1.

computation(s): the action or result of calculating or processing data (to come up with answers); thinking. Page 66.

compute: think or determine with precision. Page 98.

computed: estimated or determined by arithmetical or mathematical reckoning; calculated. Page 60.

computer: that which calculates and thinks, such as the mind. Page 139.

conceive: form an idea or concept of something in one's mind; think; imagine. Page 8.

conducive: tending to produce; contributive; helpful; favorable (usually followed by *to*). Page 105.

conduits: any means, conceived of as channels or passages, by which things are transmitted. Page 114.

CONFUSION: THE CONDITION OF AN AREA OF AN ENGRAM OR THE CONDITION OF AN ENGRAM CHAIN. INSTANTS OF EXISTENCE WHICH ARE NOT PROPERLY ALIGNED ON THE TIME TRACK. (From *LRH Glossary.*) Page 173.

connective tissue: tissue consisting mainly of fibers, fat, etc., that supports, connects and surrounds organs and other body parts. Page 156.

connotates: signifies or suggests; implies. Page 174.

conservation of energy: a law of physics that states that energy itself cannot be created and destroyed but can only alter its forms. For example, if one burned a piece of coal and collected all the smoke, ash and other particles which radiated from the burning and weighed them, one would have the same weight as before the coal was burned. Page 8.

conservatism: the tendency to preserve what is established and existing; the inclination to limit change. Page 10.

considerable: a rather large or great amount. Page 98.

consists: is made up or composed (usually followed by *of*). Page 18.

consolidating: making solid or firm; solidifying; strengthening. Page 13.

consort: to keep company or associate with. Page 166.

contagion: the transmission or communication of a disease from body to body. Hence, by extension, the transference and spreading of harmful or corrupting influences, feelings, emotions, etc., from person to person or among a number of people. Page 107.

contemplating: thinking or considering attentively or thoughtfully; considering carefully and in detail. Page 13.

contemporary: characteristic of some time period. Page 70.

contest: 1. struggle; fight. Likened to a race, game, etc., in which individuals or teams compete with one another to determine a winner. Page 10.

2. to struggle or fight against. Page 43.

control system, central: central nervous system, consisting of a brain and spinal cord. It functions as the control center of the nervous system by receiving information from the senses and sending impulses to muscles and other parts of the body that trigger the required actions. Page 9.

convulsion: a violent shaking of the body or limbs caused by uncontrollable muscle contractions. Page 131.

coordinative: that *coordinates,* makes the parts of something work together in sequence or in time with one another. Page 19.

cosmic election: *cosmic* means of or relating to the world or universe regarded as an orderly, harmonious system. *Election* means the act or power of choosing, such as the choice by God of individuals for favor or salvation. Hence, *cosmic election* means the selection or choice of someone or something by an orderly, universal system or higher power, often with an end or purpose in mind. Page 10.

costs, at all: whatever effort is needed; in spite of all losses; whatever happens. Page 81.

counter-: a word used in combination with another with the meaning of against, in opposition or response to; opposite. Page 117.

counterpart: something that corresponds to or closely resembles another, as in form or function. Page 39.

course: a particular manner or proceeding. Also, a chosen path of activity, as in *"such a course may occasionally be pursued in the entrance of a case."* Page 175.

course, a matter of: something which is to be expected as following the natural course or order of things. Page 160.

course, of: 1. naturally; without any doubt; certainly. Used to show that something written or stated is not surprising or is generally known or accepted, as in *"That book was, of course,* Dianetics: The Modern Science of Mental Health." Page vii.
2. used to point out a possibility that somebody may not have considered, as in *"unless, of course, it rested on a former engram."* Page 44.

course of, in the: while doing; during the progress or length of. Page 69.

CROSS-ENGRAM: THE SEVERE ENGRAMIC EXPERIENCE WHEREIN TWO ENGRAM CHAINS HAVE MET, CAUSING A MARKED CHANGE IN THE LIFE OF THE INDIVIDUAL. THIS IS AN ENGRAM WHICH IS ON THE TIME TRACK OF EACH OF TWO OR MORE CHAINS. (From *LRH Glossary.*) Page 142.

culminated: ended or arrived at a final stage; resulted in, often with the sense of having reached a most intense or decisive moment in the development or resolution of something. Page 1.

cure(ing): the action of solving a problem or dealing with a situation in a way that corrects or eliminates it. Page 7.

cursorily: in passing; without great attention to details. Page 17.

decimal: using the number ten as a base and counted or ordered in units of ten; or belonging to a system organized in this way. For example, 2.1, 2.2, 2.3, 2.4, 2.5, 2.6, 2.7, 2.8, 2.9, 3.0 is based on a decimal system, as ten numbers are used in order to count from 2.0 to 3.0. Page 60.

deduced: formed as a conclusion from things already observed or known. Page 26.

deism: a belief in God based on reason rather than revelation (a showing or revealing of a divine truth), and involving the view that God has set the universe and its laws in motion but does not interfere with it nor the operation of those laws. Deism was especially influential in the seventeenth and eighteenth centuries. Page 8.

delineated: described or explained in detail; outlined with precision. Page 1.

delusions: persistent false beliefs or opinions that are resistant to reason and confrontation with actual fact. Page 72.

demarked: marked so as to set apart clearly and distinctly as if by definite limits or boundaries. Page 25.

denote: signify, mean, refer to or be a mark or sign of; indicate. Page 11.

denoted: given a name with a specified meaning. Page 59.

depressant: causing or tending to cause *depression,* a lowering or lessening of one's spirits, hopes or the like. Page 110.

derange: disturb the order or arrangement of; upset the normal condition or functioning of. Also disturb mentally. Page 20.

deranged: put out of order; disordered; disarranged. Page 17.

derangement: disturbance of the function or condition of something, such as the mind. Page 155.

derivation: the action of obtaining (a conclusion, answer, etc.) from a source. Also, the action of arriving at by reasoning. Page 8.

despondency: a condition of extreme discouragement, dejection, depression or hopelessness. Page 81.

determinism: the action of causing, affecting or controlling. Page 19.

deterministic: of or relating to determinism. *See also* **determinism.** Page 19.

detriment: damage, disadvantage or harm. Page 100.

developed: presented or revealed in stages; unfolded, as in *"When an engram is located and developed."* Page 59.

deviation(s): a turning aside from something, as behavior, conduct or the like that is viewed as ideal. Page 34.

diagnostic: identifying or used in identifying; used in *diagnosis,* the process of determining by examination the nature, cause or circumstances of something. Page 45.

DIANETICIST: AN AUDITOR OF DIANETIC THERAPY. (From *LRH Glossary.*)

DIANETICS: DERIVED FROM THE GREEK WORD FOR THOUGHT, *DIANOIA.* A TERM EMPLOYED TO EMBRACE THE SCIENCE OF THOUGHT AND INCLUDING A FAMILY OF SUB-SCIENCES BY WHICH THE INDIVIDUAL AND COLLECTIVE ACTIVITIES OF MANKIND MAY BE UNDERSTOOD AND PREDICTED AND BETTERED. (From *LRH Glossary.*) Page vii.

Dickens: a reference to the writings of English author Charles Dickens (1812–1870), who was known for creating a wide range of comic, pleasant and villainous characters. Page 73.

dictates: guiding rules or principles that govern how one behaves. Page 106.

diluted: literally, made thinner or less concentrated as by adding water. Hence, reduced or lessened in force, strength, purity or brilliance, especially by mixing with something else. Page 7.

dire: characterized by severe, serious or desperate circumstances; very bad. Page 108.

disability: the inability to pursue an occupation or perform services for wages during a time period because of physical impairment such as injury received on the job, in time of war, etc. Page 1.

discharges: relieves something of things that are unneeded or unwanted as by removing them, getting rid of them or the like. Page 117.

dis-coordinated: no longer coordinated; made or caused to be uncoordinated. *Coordinate* means make the parts of something work together in sequence or in time with one another and *dis-* means not, or the reversal of some action. Page 19.

discounted: disregarded as not significant or valuable (for a particular purpose). Page 68.

discrepancies: differences between things that should correspond or match. *"Discrepancies of conduct"* would be actions or behavior that did not agree or were not consistent with the situation or condition in which a person found himself or herself. Page 143.

disheartening: depressing the hope, courage or spirits of; discouraging. Page 141.

disintegrated: having little or no *integration,* the organization of various traits, feelings, attitudes, etc., into one coordinated, harmonious personality. Page 127.

DISPERSAL: THE ACTION OF A DYNAMIC OR PURPOSE MEETING AN ENGRAM. IT IS DESCRIBABLE BY AN ANALOGY OF AN ELECTRON STREAM STRIKING IMPEDANCE AND SHOWERING AROUND IT, MUCH WEAKENED. (From *LRH Glossary.*) Page 49.

dispersion: the act or process of scattering or driving off in different directions. Page 22.

dissimulation: the act of disguising or concealing the truth of something under a pretended or false assertion, appearance, etc. Page 116.

divergence: a difference between two or more things. Page 174.

doctrine: a particular principle, position or policy taught or advocated by some political, scientific or philosophic group. Page 130.

doctrine of "automatic determinism," the: the belief that action, thought, imagination, creativity, etc., is caused by stimulus-response; that is, a certain stimulus (something that rouses a person or thing to activity or that produces a reaction in the body) automatically giving a certain response. This doctrine was exemplified by Ivan Petrovich Pavlov (1849–1936), Russian physiologist, noted for his dog experiments. Pavlov presented food (stimulus) to a dog, while he sounded a bell (also a stimulus). After repeating this procedure several times, the dog (in anticipation) would salivate at the sound of the bell, whether or not food was presented. Pavlov concluded that all acquired habits, even the higher mental activity of Man, depended on such stimulus-response. Page 130.

dramatis personae: in Dianetics it refers to the people present in an engram. *Dramatis personae* is Latin and literally means people (or persons) of a drama, used to refer to the actors or characters in a drama or play or those who are part of an actual event. Page 148.

dramatization(s): an instance of acting out; expressing oneself in a dramatic manner. Hence, a *destructive dramatization* is the acting out of a destructive experience contained in the reactive mind. Dramatization is covered more fully later, Chapter Sixteen, Dramatization. Page 34.

dream (data): something conceived of or devised (in the mind). Hence, *dream data* is data conceived of (as opposed to observed in the environment) by the individual. Page 115.

drive: an inner urge that stimulates activity; energy and initiative. Page 11.

due: as much as is required; enough; adequate. Page 94.

dynamic: from the Greek *dunamikos,* powerful. Hence, motivating or energizing force (of existence or life) as in *Dynamic Principle of Existence*. Page 1.

Dynamic: the dynamic thrust into time and space of an individual, a species, or a unit of matter or energy. Especially defined, for the purpose of Dianetics, as "Survive!" (From *LRH Glossary*.) Page 11.

Dynamic Dianetics: the science of the basic dynamics of the individual and his basic personality. At this writing, that branch of Dianetics most intensely under observation and research is this one. (From *LRH Glossary*.) Page 17.

eccentricities: deviations from what is ordinary or customary, as in conduct or manner; oddities. Page 73.

echelon: a level, as in a steplike arrangement or order. An *echelon* is one of a series in a field of activity. From the French word *echelon* meaning rung of a ladder. Page 113.

educative: pertaining to *education,* the process of training and developing the knowledge, skill, mind, character, etc., especially by formal schooling, teaching, experience. Page 27.

eidetic: of or relating to visual images recalled or reproduced that are vivid and lifelike with almost photographic accuracy. Page 97.

election, cosmic: *cosmic* means of or relating to the world or universe regarded as an orderly, harmonious system. *Election* means the act or power of choosing, such as the choice by God of individuals for favor or salvation. Hence, *cosmic election* means the selection or choice of someone or something by an orderly, universal system or higher power, often with an end or purpose in mind. Page 10.

electric shock(s): the firing of 180 to 460 volts of electricity through the brain from temple to temple or from the front to the back of one side of the head. It causes a severe convulsion (uncontrollable shaking of the body) or seizure (unconsciousness and inability to control movements of the body) of long duration. Page 54.

electrons: minute, negatively charged particles that form a part of all atoms. Page 107.

elicit: draw out, cause or produce something as a reaction or response. Page 94.

elude: escape, avoid or evade, as if by quickness, deception, etc. Page 98.

embrace: include or contain as part of a whole. Page 1.

E-Meter: a specially designed instrument used by a trained auditor. The full name is electropsychometer, from *electro* (electricity), *psyche* (soul) and *meter* (measure), an electronic device for measuring the mental state or change of state of Homo sapiens. It is not a lie detector. It does not diagnose or cure anything. It is used by auditors to assist the preclear in locating areas of spiritual distress or travail.

emote: express emotion. Page 95.

employ: apply (a thing) to some definite purpose; use as a means to achieve something. Page 66.

encephalograph: an instrument for measuring and recording the electrical activity of the brain. Page 88.

encompass: include or contain something. Page vii.

end: final state or condition; result or outcome. Page 1.

engage: to attract and hold the attention of a person or persons. Page 106.

engaged (on): entered upon doing, or being occupied with, some activity. Page 105.

ENGRAM: A PERIOD OF PHYSICAL PAIN INCLUDING UNCONSCIOUSNESS AND ANTAGONISM EXPERIENCED BY AN INDIVIDUAL, GROUP OR SOCIETY AND RESIDING THEREAFTER AS IRRATIONAL AND RESTIMULATABLE DRAMATIZATIONS. (From *LRH Glossary.*) Page 36.

ENGRAM CHAIN: A SERIES OF SIMILAR ENGRAMS ON ONE OR MORE DYNAMICS WHICH IMPEDE THE DYNAMICS OF THE INDIVIDUAL. (From *LRH Glossary.*) Much like the interlinking rings of a metal chain, a series of similar engrams are connected to each other in a chain. The subject of engram chains is covered in Chapter Fifteen, Engram Chains. Page 44.

ENGRAM LOCK: AN ENGRAM, SEVERE IN ITS OWN RIGHT, SUCCEEDING A BASIC ENGRAM ON ANY ENGRAM CHAIN. (From *LRH Glossary.*) Page 65.

ensuing: following afterward; next in time. Page 42.

entangle: literally, cause to become *tangled,* twisted together into a confused mass, as of strands, threads or the like. Figuratively, cause to become involved in problems, confusions, complications, etc. Page 26.

entered upon: started on (a road, path, etc.) or along some course of action. Page 79.

entities: things (or beings) that have real, independent, separate or self-contained existence or identity; things that exist as a particular unit. Page 13.

entity, perceptic: a self-contained bundle of received perceptions such as smell, taste, sight, sound, touch, etc. Page 39.

equation: a mathematics term showing that two things are of the same value or equal each other. Also, by extension, any situation or problem with several variable factors that has been calculated and proven with mathematical precision. Page vii.

equivocal: of uncertain nature or classification. Page 54.

eradicating: removing or eliminating something completely. Page 69.

erase: remove or eliminate completely. Page 17.

essence, in: basically or fundamentally. Page 67.

eugenic: of or having to do with *eugenics,* the study or belief in the possibility of improving a species (or population) through the eradication of hereditary traits considered undesirable. Page 107.

euphoria: a feeling of well-being or happiness, especially one that is groundless or inappropriate to current circumstances. Page 121.

evaluate: consider or examine something to judge its importance, extent, quality or condition. Page 8.

evolution: the idea that all living things evolved from simple organisms and changed through the ages to produce millions of different species; the theory that development of a species or organism from its original or primitive state to its present state includes adaptation (form or structure modified to fit a changed environment). Page 10.

evolve: 1. work out or develop especially by experience, experimentation or intensive care or effort. Page viii.
2. develop from an earlier biological form or develop a characteristic in this way. Page 25.

exaggerated: made to appear more noticeable or prominent than is usual or desirable. Page 72.

exert: 1. to put forth or put out (as strength, power or effort); set in operation. Page 40.
2. to bring (as a force or influence) into effect, especially with lasting and sustained effort. Page 94.

exhaustion: the act or process of *exhausting,* drawing out or draining off completely. Page 46.

exhaustive: leaving no part unexamined or unconsidered; complete; thorough. Page viii.

experimental psychology: the experimental study of the response of a person or animal to stimuli. *Experimental* means based on testing, for the purpose of finding something out. *Stimuli* (plural of *stimulus*) are actions or agents that cause or change an activity in an organism, organ or part, such as food that is put before a rat stimulates the rat to move toward it. In 1879, German professor Wilhelm Wundt (1832–1920), who conceived that Man was an animal without a soul, founded one of the first laboratories of experimental psychology, at Leipzig University. Page 155.

extended: stretched out so as to have a greater scope, range, reach or the like. For example, someone who hears sounds far louder or sees images far sharper or brighter than what is considered normal has extended hearing or vision. Page 47.

extension: the state of being *extended. See* **extended**. Page 47.

exterior-world: the sphere of human activity outside that of the mind such as objects, environments and events. Page 168.

extraneous: not constituting a vital element or part. Page 113.

facet: any one of several parts or sides of something; particular aspect of a thing. Page 11.

facility: ability to do something with ease or skill. Page 50.

fad: a temporary fashion, notion, manner of conduct, etc., especially one followed enthusiastically by a group. Page 86.

faith healing: healing accomplished through prayer or religious faith. Page 166.

fanatic: a person marked or motivated by an extreme, unreasoning enthusiasm, as for a cause. Page 150.

far from: very different from being. Page 166.

fetus: the unborn human in the womb, from after the second month of pregnancy until birth. Page 47.

finite: 1. subject to limitation or conditions, such as those of space, time, circumstances and the laws of the physical universe. Page 8. 2. fixed, determined or definite, as in *"The why of the goal may lie above the finite line. But below it—demarked by the word 'Survive!'—definite manifestations are visible."* Page 25.

first place, in the: firstly; first in order. The phrase is used to give a fact or reason of primary importance that proves or strengthens what is being stated. Page 79.

fit: a sudden outburst of emotion. Page 46.

fixed person: a person who is regarded highly and who, as a result, exercises a strong influence on another, such that the latter could be said to be fixated on the person, for example, a parent, relative or someone else from the preclear's past. *Fixated* means being stuck on or overly attached to someone or something. Page 94.

flagrant: shockingly noticeable or evident; obvious; glaring. Page 73.

flank: the extreme right or left side of an army, fleet, etc. To attack an enemy in the flank means to attack them on the side, a common military tactic as it is generally a weak point of defense. Page 95.

flicking out: removing from a place or area as if by means of a quick, light tap. Page 121.

follower: a later engram on a chain. Page 96.

folly: foolish action, practice, idea, etc. Page 151.

forebear(s): a member of past generations, as of a group or race. Page 10.

foreign: not natural to the person or thing specified; not belonging. Page 70.

forgetter mechanism: the hypnotist uses the forgetter mechanism with most of his suggestions. With the forgetter mechanism, the patient is unable to recall whether he had ever been hypnotized or not. For example: A man is placed in a hypnotic trance by standard hypnotic technique or some hypnotic drug. The operator then may say to him, "When you awaken, there is something you must do. Whenever I touch my tie, you will remove your coat. When I let go of my tie, you will put on your coat. Now you will forget that I have told you to do this." The subject is then awakened. He is not consciously aware of the command. If told he had been given an order while "asleep," he would resist the idea or shrug, but he would not know. The operator then touches his tie. The subject may make some remark about its being too warm and so take his coat off. The operator then releases his tie. The subject may remark that he is now cold and will put his coat back on. See *Dianetics: The Modern Science of Mental Health*. Page 69.

formulated: worked out or formed in one's mind; devised or developed, as a method, system, etc. Page 1.

for the purposes of: what is needed in a particular situation. Also, the intention, aim or function of something; the thing that something is supposed to achieve. Page 20.

frontal lobe: the region at the front and top left or right side of the brain. A *lobe* is a roundish projection or division, as of an organ of the body. Page 11.

fruitless: producing no effect or result; useless. Page 97.

full, to its: to the greatest extent; thoroughly. Page 94.

fumbly: marked by clumsiness; inefficient or unskillful. Page 132.

fuse: a device to protect against shock, overload, etc. From the field of electricity where in an electric circuit, a strip of metal is inserted, which melts (or "blows") and thus interrupts the electrical flow to prevent damage should the electrical current increase beyond a certain safe level. Page 22.

genetic: having to do with *genes,* the basic units of the physical body capable of transmitting characteristics from one generation to the next. Page 156.

geometrical progression: a series of numbers, such as 1/8, 1/4, 1/2, 1, 2, 4, 8, 16, 32, 64, 128, etc., where each number is multiplied by a constant quantity (in this example, by 2) to arrive at the next number. This results in each next number changing by greater and greater amounts as the progression advances. Page 147.

germane: truly relevant; closely connected. Page 105.

gland(s): a mass of cells or an organ in the body that produces particular chemical substances for use in the body. For example, adrenal glands produce adrenaline, a hormone that is released into the bloodstream in response to physical or mental stress, as from fear of injury. It initiates many bodily responses, including stimulation of heart action and increase in blood pressure. Page 66.

glandular: of or pertaining to glands. Page 1.

glandular secretion: the act or process of a gland producing and releasing a *secretion,* a chemical substance that fulfills some function within an organism. Page 18.

gradation(s): any process or change taking place through a series of stages, by degrees or in a gradual manner. Page 9.

grade: a degree or step in a scale, as of quality, value or quantity. For instance, first-grade would be the best or most of something, second-grade would be less and third-grade would be thought of as much less. Page 10.

graduated scale: a scale of condition graduated from zero to infinity. The word *graduated* is meant to define lessening or increasing degrees of condition. The difference between one point on a graduated scale and another point could be as different or as wide as the entire range of the scale itself, or it could be so tiny as to need the most minute discernment (ability to perceive the difference) for its establishment. Page 59.

groundswell: any surge of support, approval or enthusiasm, especially among the general public. A *groundswell* is literally a broad, deep swell or rolling of the sea, due to a distant storm. Page vii.

guardian: a person who is entrusted by law with the care of someone, as a child. Page 95.

guile: particular skill and cleverness in dealing with sensitive or difficult matters. Page 96.

gulf: a wide gap, as in position, understanding, etc. Page 86.

hatpins: long, ornamental pins for fastening a woman's hat to her hair. Page 159.

hectic: characterized by intense excitement, activity or agitation, sometimes accompanied by rapid movement. Page 150.

heed: careful or close attention; notice; observation (usually with give or take). Page 67.

heir: one to whom something, such as a tradition or culture, a natural talent, a quality of character, is transmitted, as from his ancestors. Page 10.

hence: for this reason; as a result. Page 20.

heretofore: before this time; up until now. Page 129.

heuristic(ally): (in a manner that involves) using experimentation, evaluation or trial-and-error methods; involving investigation and conclusions based on invariable workability. Page 1.

his: those who belong to him; his family, friends, etc., as in *"destructive to himself and to his."* Page 34.

hitherto: up to this time; until now. Page 70.

hormones: chemical substances produced by glands in the body that regulate growth and development, control the function of various tissues, support reproductive functions and regulate metabolism (the process used to break down food to create energy). Page 47.

human anatomy: a person's body. Page 155.

hypnosis: a sleeplike condition that can be artificially induced in people by another, in which they can respond to questions and are very susceptible to suggestions. Page 47.

hypothetical: based on something tentatively accepted, assumed or supposed, to provide a basis for some action, belief, etc. Page 89.

hysterias: states of extreme or exaggerated emotion such as excitement or panic. Page 68.

"I": (in philosophy and other fields) the source of thinking; the person himself, as distinct from the body, who is aware of being self. Page 114.

identity(ies): **1.** the characteristics and qualities of a specific person or thing; individuality. Page 40.
2. of or pertaining to exact samenesses in qualities or characteristics; of equivalents or equals. *Identity-thought* is A=A=A. Identity thinking is further described in Chapter Eight, The Character of Engrams. Page 66.

if only: used to express a reason for something, even if not the only or best of the possible reasons. Page 113.

illusion(s): a perception that represents what is perceived in a way different from the way it is in reality. Page 72.

illustration: something which sheds light upon, makes clear or explains (such as by examples, comparisons, etc.). Page 113.

immeasurably: in a way that is *immeasurable,* too large or too much to be measured; immensely. Page 122.

immediacy: the state or quality of being *immediate,* occurring or responding instantly and without delay. Page 114.

immortality: endless life or existence. Page 9.

impedance: the opposition in a circuit to the flow of electric current (moving electrons). Page 181.

impede(s): hinder in movement or progress such as by obstacles or barriers. Page 13.

impinged: came in contact with; had an effect or impact on. Page 108.

implanted: fixed, established or embedded securely, as in the mind or consciousness. Page 42.

implicit(ly): (in a way that is) not affected by any doubt or uncertainty. Page 128.

imposed: put or established by, or as if by, authority. Page 42.

impunity: exemption from penalty or harm. Page 166.

inanimate: not having the qualities associated with active, living organisms; not alive. Page 10.

incapacitating: depriving of ability or strength; making incapable or unfit; disabling. Page 68.

incident (to): accompanying something or occurring as a consequence of it. Page 27.

incredulity: the state or action of being unable or unwilling to believe. Page 117.

incumbent upon: resting upon as a duty or obligation. Page 116.

indiscriminate: not making careful choices or distinctions; lacking in selectivity. Page 67.

induced: brought about, produced or caused. Page 116.

indulging: giving way to; allowing to occur without restraint. Page 68.

in evidence: plainly evident; attracting notice or attention. Page 160.

inexhaustible: that cannot be entirely used up. Page 42.

infatuation: a great, often temporary and irrational passion (intense feelings, emotions or love) for somebody or something. Page 82.

infective: producing *infection,* the reproduction and spreading of germs or bacteria in the body. Page 47.

infestation: the state of being overrun in large numbers and in a way that becomes threatening, harmful or unpleasant. Page 70.

infiltrated: (of something harmful) penetrated or entered an area, substance, group, etc., as if by spreading over or passing into. Page 148.

inflicted: caused or given to someone, as pain, wounds, injuries or the like. Page 44.

inherent(ly): (in a way or manner that is) existing in someone or something as a natural and inseparable quality or characteristic. Page 27.

in lieu of: in place of; instead of. Page 183.

innate: relating to qualities that a person is born with. Page 69.

innocuous: not hurtful or injurious; harmless. Page 167.

in order to: as a means to; with the purpose of. Page 1.

in other words: put differently; otherwise stated, often used to introduce an explanation of something and usually in a simpler way. Page 26.

in short: introducing a summary statement of what has been previously stated in a few words; in summary. Page 34.

insofar as: to such an extent, to such a degree. Page 54.

in some way: in an unspecified manner; somehow. Page 108.

insulin shock(s): a form of psychiatric shock treatment introduced in the 1930s, consisting of injecting an excessive amount of insulin (a hormone regulating the level of sugar in the blood) into the body, thereby inducing convulsions and coma. Page 54.

integration: the organization of various traits, feelings, attitudes, etc., into one coordinated, harmonious personality. Page 33.

in terms of: in relation to; with reference to. Page 26.

in that: because; it being the case that. Used after a statement to explain or give an example. Page 27.

in the course of: while doing; during the progress or length of. Page 69.

in the first place: firstly; first in order. The phrase is used to give a fact or reason of primary importance that proves or strengthens what is being stated. Page 79.

intimidated: forced into, or inhibited from, some action by fear (of someone else's actions, personality, etc.). Page 81.

intricate: having many interwinding, intermeshing or interrelating parts, phases, patterns or elements. Page 19.

introverts: turns (the mind, thought, etc.) inwards upon itself. Page 67.

in (its) turn: one thing coming after another. Page vii.

invalidating: depriving something of its force, value or effectiveness; making less of or nothing of. Page 167.

inverse ratio: the ratio (proportionate relationship) of two quantities which vary inversely (*inverse* is opposite to or reversing something); that is, one increases in the exact proportion as the other decreases. Page 122.

involuntary muscles: muscles that act independently and not under the conscious will of the person. These muscles are responsible for actions such as heartbeat, intestinal contractions, etc. Page 18.

key(ed) into: literally, keys are small manual devices for opening and closing or switching electronic contacts, used here to describe how a dormant engram can be activated and thrown into circuit. Page 42.

keynote: the central or most important point or theme of something. Page 26.

keys: *keys* are tabs or an index of categories, used here with the sense of something which identifies. Also, in electronics, keys are small manual devices for opening and closing or switching electronic contacts. Used as an analogy of the mind to describe *perceptic keys* in an engram which when unanalytically perceived by the individual in his environment, may in greater or lesser degrees set the engram into reaction. Page 42.

kingdoms, (three): three broad divisions of natural objects: the animal, vegetable and mineral kingdoms. A *kingdom* is a region or sphere of nature. Page 8.

law(s): a statement of fact, based on observation, that a particular natural or scientific phenomenon (event, circumstance or experience that can be sensed) always occurs if certain conditions are present. Page 1.

length, at: after some time; eventually. Page 104.

libidos: *(psychoanalysis)* supposed manifestations of the sexual drive, specifically as viewed by Sigmund Freud (1856–1939), who originated the theory that the energy or urges motivating behavior are largely sexual in origin. Page 48.

lies (in): is found; consists or is based on (usually followed by *in*). Page 7.

lift: 1. loosen and (begin to) remove, as if from some surrounding material. Page 96.

2. raise or be raised to a higher position or level. Page 104.

line(s): 1. an indication of an identifiable separation of things; boundary, as in *"Conceiving this split as a line drawn through* *the area, we can assign a* Dynamic Principle of Existence *to all that data remaining in the Knowable field."* Page 8.

2. direction, course of action or thought, sphere of activity, as in *"It can then be subdivided specifically into several dynamic lines as applicable to each form or species."* Page 26.

3. a group of things arranged, or thought of as arranged, in a row or series, as in *"If one is accidentally skipped, the third in line will be found to hold or sag."* Page 105.

Lock: A PERIOD OF MENTAL ANGUISH DEPENDING FOR ITS FORCE UPON AN ENGRAM. IT MAY OR MAY NOT BE AVAILABLE TO THE ANALYTICAL MIND, BUT IT DOES NOT CONTAIN ACTUAL UNCONSCIOUSNESS. (From *LRH Glossary.*) From an old English word *loc,* meaning bolt, bar, a mechanism used to fasten something to another thing. Page 45.

loop(s): a redoubling of the time track back on itself. In this case incidents are not in their correct place on the time track. Page 173.

lowest common denominator: the most fundamental factor held in common by a number of people or things. Page 8.

lull: cause something to become less active. Page 118.

lump sum: an amount of money that is given in a single payment, rather than being divided into smaller periodic payments. Page 1.

magnitude: the quantity or greatness of size, extent, importance or influence. Page 48.

maladjustment(s): instances of inability to adjust to the demands of the environment, interpersonal relationships and the stresses of daily living. Page 48.

malady: an illness or sickness. Also, a condition or situation that is undesirable and unwholesome and requires a remedy. Page 46.

Man: the human race or species, humankind, Mankind. Page 1.

man: a human being, without regard to sex or age; a person. Page 13.

manic: a person characterized by *mania,* abnormal excitability, exaggerated feelings of well-being, etc. Page 150.

manifest: to make something evident by showing or demonstrating it very clearly. Page 56.

markedly: in a manner that is strikingly obvious and clearly defined; to a significant extent; noticeably. Page 122.

mask: a covering for the mouth and nose used, before surgical operations, to administer drugs that a person inhales, which produce insensitivity to pain and loss of consciousness, etc. Page 45.

materially: to a great extent; substantially; considerably. Page 70.

matter, no: regardless of; it is of no importance. Page 43.

matter of course, a: something which is to be expected as following the natural course or order of things. Page 160.

maze: any complex system or arrangement that causes bewilderment or confusion. Page 117.

mechanism(s): 1. the agency or means by which an effect is produced or a purpose is accomplished, likened to the structure or system of parts in a mechanical device for carrying out some function or doing something, as in *"Certain mechanisms, such as 'Forget it,' may swerve a minimally painful or unconscious experience off the time track."* Page 65.
2. a structure or system (of parts, components, etc.) that together perform a particular function as would occur in a machine, as in *"The organism possesses many inherent mechanisms and abilities by which it can learn or preserve or forward itself along the dynamic."* Page 72.

members: parts of the body; limbs such as arms or legs. Page 49.

menace: something that is a possible source of danger or harm. Page 67.

mere: just what is specified and nothing more. Page 9.

merely: only what is being referred to and nothing more; just; simply. Page 69.

ministrations: acts or instances of care, aid and service given (such as during childbirth). Page 160.

more or less: to an undetermined degree; to some extent; somewhat. Page 45.

motor: of, pertaining to or involving muscular movement. Page 18.

motor strip: a long, narrow area of the brain which is believed to control the movement of the various muscles and movements of the body. *Motor* means of, relating to or being a nerve that passes from the central nervous system to a muscle, conducting an impulse that causes movement. Page 88.

mutation: a sudden structural change in the hereditary material of an organism's cells resulting in a new trait or characteristic not found in the parents, as distinguished from a variation resulting from generations of gradual change. *Hereditary* means having to do with traits or characteristics transmitted from generation to generation through reproduction. Page 8.

native: belonging to a person by birth or to a thing by nature. Page 150.

natural selection: the process by which forms of life having traits that better enable them to adapt to specific environmental pressures such as predators, changes in climate, competition for food or mates, will tend to survive and reproduce in greater numbers than others of their kind, thus ensuring the perpetuation of those favorable traits in succeeding generations. A *predator* is an animal that hunts, kills and eats other animals in order to survive, or any other organism that behaves in a similar manner. Page 8.

nature: 1. kind or sort, as in *"All errors of a psychic or psychosomatic nature can be considered, for the purposes of this analogy, to lie in the reactive mind."* Page 20.
2. the essential characteristics and qualities of a thing, as in *"It is the content of the engram which causes the aberration and forms its nature."* Page 53.
3. the world, including all forces and processes that produce and control its phenomena. *"It* [the Tone Scale] *is not arbitrary, but will be found to approximate some actual governing law in nature."* Page 59.

nebulous: lacking definite form or limits; not clearly defined or described. Page 1.

necessity: something that is necessary and that one cannot live without, such as air, food, water, etc.; also an unavoidable need or compulsion to do something. Page 8.

nervous breakdown: a severe emotional disorder, especially when occurring suddenly and often marked by great sadness, depression, anxiety, etc., disabling one's ability to function normally in life. Page 142.

nervous system: the network of nerve cells, tissues, spinal cord, etc., in humans that carries sensations to the brain and impulses to organs and muscles. Page 18.

neurasthenia, post-battle: a condition, *neurasthenia,* marked by fatigue, irritability, weakness, anxiety, etc., often occurring in soldiers after combat duty. Page 142.

neuroses: plural of *neurosis,* an emotional state containing conflicts and emotional data inhibiting the abilities or welfare of the individual. Page 1.

New Thought: literally, any of various philosophical and religious movements such as the New Thought movement (late 1800s) and its offshoots, holding that affirmative thought or the adoption of a favorable mental attitude results in beneficial changes in Man. Their workable optimism was in contrast with the "old thought" of sin, evil and pessimistic resignation. Hence, *"the thinker of the New Thought,"* an individual or group that brings new, independent and constructive philosophic or religious insight or principles to Mankind. Page 10.

1938: in 1938 L. Ron Hubbard wrote the manuscript entitled *Excalibur,* a work which, though unpublished, contained information that has since been released in Dianetics and Scientology materials, including his discovery that the lowest common denominator of existence is "Survive!" *Excalibur* was the name of the magic sword of King Arthur, a legendary king in England said to have brought peace and justice in ancient times. Page 1.

nitrous oxide: a sweet-smelling, sweet-tasting gas used in dentistry and surgery to put the patient into unconsciousness. Page 44.

noble: having or showing qualities of high moral character, such as courage, generosity or honor. Page 79.

no matter: regardless of; it is of no importance. Page 43.

nomenclature: a set or system of names or terms, as those used in a particular science or art. Page v.

nominated: called by, assigned or given a name. Page 18.

non-aberrative: not causing or producing aberration. Page 27.

non-pathologic: not involving, not caused by, or not of the nature of a disease. Page 116.

notation(s): literally, a note of something as an aid to memory, a record of experiences or the like. Used figuratively in reference to a record in the mind. Page 120.

null: in electronics, indicating a reading of zero when a measured quantity is undetectable or at a minimum. Hence, descriptive of a condition in which something is ineffective, incapable of functioning or the like. Page 49.

null(ify): take away the effectiveness of something; make something be of little or no value, effect or importance. Page 117.

obstetricians: doctors who specialize in *obstetrics,* the branch of medical science concerned with childbirth and caring for and treating women in, or in connection with, childbirth. Page 160.

obtains: is in force or effect; prevails. Page 47.

occasion: cause; bring about. Page 22.

of course: 1. naturally; without any doubt; certainly. Used to show that something written or stated is not surprising or is generally known or accepted, as in *"That book was, of course,* Dianetics: The Modern Science of Mental Health." Page vii.
2. used to point out a possibility that somebody may not have considered, as in *"unless, of course, it rested on a former engram."* Page 44.

olfactory: having to do with the sense of smell. Page 39.

on record: existing and set down in some preserved form and available for viewing, such as by the public. Page 171.

on the order of: resembling to some extent; like. Page 120.

on the part of: with regard or respect to the one (or ones) specified. Page 22.

operating on: performing or exerting a function with or on someone, as in *"The analyst might even experience relief from operating on patients, since it might clarify his own locks."* Page 166.

operator: the person who hypnotizes another. *See also* **hypnosis.** Page 43.

optimum: of or pertaining to the point at which the condition, degree or amount of something is the most favorable or advantageous to the attainment of some end. Page 43.

orangewood stick: a slender, rounded stick with tapered ends of hard, fine-grained wood from the orange tree, used for manicuring the nails. Page 159.

orders: 1. classes defined by the common attributes of their members; kinds. Lower orders would include members at various levels of living things, animal or vegetable, in contrast to humans, as in *"Energy in its various forms is the primary motivator in the lower orders."* Page 19.

2. classes, groups, kinds or sorts of things having rank in a scale of excellence or importance, or distinguished from others by nature or character, as in *"The theory of 'determinism by stimuli and experience' is true of the lower orders of command mechanisms, as it is in animals."* Page 113.

organic: relating to or affecting organs or an organ of the body (such as a brain, kidney, eye, heart or lung). Page 39.

organic sensation: the sense that tells the central nervous system the condition of the organism or the various organs of the body. Page 39.

organism: 1. an organized living body, especially any living matter such as a plant, animal or bacteria. Page 9.

2. any complex (living) thing or system having properties and functions determined not only by the properties and relations of its individual parts, but by the character of the whole that they compose. Page 48.

originated: brought into being; created or initiated. Page 39.

out of: 1. from among, as in *"were rehabilitated, twenty out of twenty."* Page 1.

2. from an origin or source, as in *"will elicit replies straight out of his principal engrams."* Page 94.

3. from within; indicates something being removed from a place, as in *"The analyzer is quite adept at throwing out of itself erroneous data."* Page 116.

out of circuit: literally, disconnected. From an electrical term meaning switched off and not part of a circuit supplying electrical power. A *circuit* is a complete route traveled by an electric current and which carries out a specific action, such as supplying electricity to a light bulb. Page 22.

outrageously: shockingly excessive or bad; exceeding all bounds of reasonableness. Page 115.

overlaid: laid or spread over or across so as to cover. Page 48.

paced: literally, moved with steady, regular steps along some path or way; hence, figuratively, caused to proceed along a route or course at a steady, regular rate. Page 129.

parity: correspondence or similarity drawn between two things for the purpose of illustration. Page 114.

parlance: a particular way of speaking or using words, especially a way common to those with a particular job or interest. Page 121.

particular: having separate and distinct characteristics, qualities, etc., from others of the same group, category or nature; of or belonging to a single, definite thing; not general. Page 116.

particularly: **1.** especially; specifically and individually, as in *"no damage, particularly in the earlier months, is too great for the organism to reconstruct."* Page 159.
2. to a great degree, as in *"The number of prenatal engrams should not particularly appall the auditor."* Page 159.

pathologically: from *pathology,* the study of diseases. Hence, *"pathologically incompetent"* means physically injured (permanently) because of past disease. Page 48.

patients: persons under the supervision, care or treatment of someone. Page vii.

patter: talk, discussion, speech associated with a particular situation or group of persons. Page 107.

peculiar: distinctive in nature or character from all others; unique or specific to a person or thing or category. Also, different from the usual or normal; uncommon. Page 79.

perceptic: a perceived and recorded sense message, such as organic sensation, smell, taste, tactile, audio, visio, etc. Page 18.

perceptic entity: a self-contained bundle of received perceptions such as smell, taste, sight, sound, touch, etc. Page 39.

perceptive: same as *perceptic.* See **perceptic.** Page 118.

perforce: by necessity; by force of circumstance. Page 131.

perpetual: continuing or enduring forever; everlasting. Page 10.

person: the actual self or individual personality of a human being, as in *"the residence of person."* Page 22.

phenomenally: to an impressive degree; extraordinarily. Page 166.

phenomenon: (plural, *phenomena*) a thing that appears or is perceived or observed; an individual fact, occurrence or change as perceived by any of the senses or by the mind; applied chiefly to a fact or occurrence the cause or explanation of which is under observation or being scientifically described. Page 47.

philosophy: 1. a branch of knowledge or study devoted to the systematic examination of basic concepts such as truth, existence, reality and freedom. Page 1.

2. a system of motivating concepts or principles such as one that a person lives by. Page 26.

phraseology: the way in which words and phrases are used; choice and pattern of words. Page 72.

physio-animal: from *physio* meaning physical, or of the body and *animal,* a living organism that is distinguished from plants by independent movement and responsive sense organs. Hence, *physio-animal,* of or pertaining to the physical body or parts of a lower order organism than Man. The physio-animal mind is fully described in Chapter Two, An Analogy of the Mind. Page 18.

physiological: of or pertaining to *physiology,* the functions and activities of living organisms and their parts, including all physical and chemical processes. Page 17.

physiological amentia: a condition or instance characterized by lack of intellectual development or severe mental retardation from a birth defect or from damage to the brain in early childhood. *Physiological* means of or pertaining to the functions and activities of living organisms and their parts, including all physical and chemical processes. Page 54.

physiology: the functions and activities of living organisms and their parts, including all physical and chemical processes. Page 11.

pick up: to acquire or receive something, often in an unsystematic way such as merely by being near someone. Page 108.

pitch: the degree of highness or lowness of a sound or tone. Notes in music with a low pitch have a slower rate of vibration than those with a high pitch. Page 39.

plane: a level of existence, consciousness or development. Page 114.

plotted: laid out or shown (graphically), as the condition or course of something. Page 40.

polarity, reversed: that quality or condition in a physical body or system that manifests an opposite or contrasting property, as in a magnet where one end is positive and the other negative. One end is thought of as being reversed from what the other end is. Hence, *reversed polarity* refers to a state whereby one object, condition, etc., has an opposite characteristic, force, etc., to something else. Page 121.

pose(s): assert, state or put forward. Page 10.

positive: 1. explicitly laid down; expressed without qualification; beyond doubt or question. Page 65.

2. emphasizing what is hopeful or to the good; constructive. Page 105.

positive suggestion: in hypnosis, a suggestion or command which is given to a hypnotized subject who then obeys it unknowingly. Also, any phrase or command in the mind acting like one given to a hypnotized person. For example: A man is placed in a hypnotic trance by standard hypnotic technique or some hypnotic drug. The operator then may say to him, "When you awaken, there is something you must do. Whenever I touch my tie, you will remove your coat. When I let go of my tie, you will put on your coat. Now you will forget that I have told you to do this." The subject is then awakened. He is not consciously aware of the command. If told he had been given an order while "asleep," he would resist the idea or shrug, but he would not know. The operator then touches his tie. The subject may make some remark about its being too warm and so take his coat off. The operator then releases his tie. The subject may remark that he is now cold and will put his coat back on. See *Dianetics: The Modern Science of Mental Health*. Page 43.

post: a position or place where someone or something has specific duties or functions. Page 20.

post-: after; later. Page 43.

post-battle neurasthenia: a condition, *neurasthenia,* marked by fatigue, irritability, weakness, anxiety, etc., often occurring in soldiers after combat duty. Page 142.

post-hypnotic: from *post,* after and *hypnotic,* of hypnotism. Of or pertaining to the period after hypnosis; of a suggestion made during hypnosis to be effective after awakening. Page 43.

potential: capability or power, as in *"the potential of the analytical mind."* Page 40.

potentiality: the state or condition of having capability or power. Page 117.

power of choice: the ability or capacity to determine or decide something (such as a course of action). Page 113.

precariously: in a manner that is dependent upon chance or circumstances; in a way that is uncertain or insecure. Page 47.

PRECLEAR: ANY INDIVIDUAL ENTERED UPON DIANETIC THERAPY FOR THE PURPOSE OF BEING CLEARED. (From *LRH Glossary.*) Page 79.

precursors: engrams occurring earlier on a chain. (*Precursor* means something that comes before and leads to the development or existence of something later.) Engram chains are further described in Chapter Fifteen, Engram Chains. Page 45.

predominating: having greater importance or influence than something else. Page 171.

prefrontal lobotomies: psychiatric operations carried out by boring holes in the skull, entering the brain and severing the nerve pathways in the two frontal lobes, resulting in the patient becoming an emotional vegetable. Page 54.

prejudicial: causing harm or injury; damaging. Page 68.

prenatal(s): 1. occurring, existing or taking place before birth. In Dianetics it denotes experience and incidents which take place and are recorded in the mind while in the womb prior to or during birth. Page 47.

2. incidents (engrams) existing or occurring before or during birth. Page 47.

preponderance: the fact of being greater in quantity; the majority. Page 98.

presumed: taken for granted or supposed as being true in the absence of proof to the contrary. Page 44.

prevalence: the state of being widely existing or generally practiced. Page 157.

primary: that which is the first in order, rank or importance; anything from which something else arises or is derived. Page vii.

Primary Law: *primary* is that which is first in order, rank or importance; anything from which something else arises or is derived. *Law* is a statement of fact, based on observation, that a particular natural or scientific phenomenon (event, circumstance or experience that can be sensed) always occurs if certain conditions are present. In Dianetics, *Primary Law* is a reference to the first axiom, the Dynamic Principle of Existence—"Survive!"—as described in Chapter One of this book. The principle first appeared in a previous unpublished work, *Excalibur,* written by L. Ron Hubbard in 1938. Page 1.

principle: a fundamental truth, law, doctrine or motivating force, upon which others are based. Page 1.

procreating: reproducing; bringing into being; generating offspring. Page 8.

productive of: that causes or brings about; that results in. Page 46.

progeny: children, descendants or offspring considered as a group or collectively. Page 13.

promiscuity: behavior characterized by casual and indiscriminate sexual relations with a number of partners. Page 107.

prone to: likely or liable to suffer from, do or experience something, typically something regrettable or unwelcome. Page 95.

proofed: made resistant or not capable of being affected. Page 141.

proviso: a condition, qualification or limitation. Page 20.

psyche: the mind. Page 48.

psychic: of or pertaining to the mind. Page 20.

psychoanalysis: a system of mental therapy developed by Austrian physician Sigmund Freud (1856–1939) in 1894, in which the patient was made to talk about and recall for years events from his childhood, believed by Freud to be the cause of mental ills. The practitioner read significances into all statements and evaluated them for the patient (told him what to think), along sex-related lines. Page 166.

psychological: of the mind, mental. Page 160.

psychology, experimental: the experimental study of the response of a person or animal to stimuli. *Experimental* means based on testing, for the purpose of finding something out. *Stimuli* (plural of *stimulus*) are actions or agents that cause or change an activity in an organism, organ or part, such as food that is put before a rat stimulates the rat to move toward it. In 1879, German professor Wilhelm Wundt (1832–1920), who conceived that Man was an animal without a soul, founded one of the first laboratories of experimental psychology, at Leipzig University. Page 155.

psychoneurotic: of or pertaining to *psychoneurosis,* a psychiatric term for neurosis where a person expresses feelings of anxiety, obsession, etc., without apparent cause. Page 110.

psychoses: conflicts of commands which seriously reduce the individual's ability to solve his problems in his environment to a point where he cannot adjust himself to some vital phase of his environmental needs. Page 1.

psychosomatic: 1. *psycho,* of course, refers to mind and *somatic* refers to body; the term *psychosomatic* means the mind making the body ill or illnesses which have been created physically within the body by derangement of the mind. About 70 percent of the physician's current roster of diseases fall into the category of psychosomatic illness. Page 1.

2. an engram command enforced upon the body. Specifically, the analytical mind re-undergoing the experience of the engram, as in *"There is only* one *psychosomatic which is common to all engrams."*

The psychosomatic is further described in Chapter Five, Engrams. Page 49.

PURPOSE: THE SURVIVAL ROUTE CHOSEN BY AN INDIVIDUAL, A SPECIES OR A UNIT OF MATTER OR ENERGY IN THE ACCOMPLISHMENT OF ITS DYNAMIC. (NOTE: THE PURPOSE IS SPECIFIC AND MAY BE CLOSELY DEFINED BEING A SUBDIVISION OF ONE OF THE SUB-DYNAMICS. IT HAS BEEN TENTATIVELY ESTABLISHED BY INVESTIGATION THAT AN INDIVIDUAL HUMAN BEING HAS ESTABLISHED HIS PURPOSE FOR LIFE AT THE AGE OF TWO YEARS AND THAT THE ACTUAL PURPOSE IS NOT DERIVED IN ANY DEGREE FROM ENGRAMS, BUT IS ONLY WARPED BY THEM.) (From *LRH Glossary.*) Page 8.

pusillanimity: lack of courage; cowardliness. Page 34.

racial-educational: of, relating to or based on factors of race or education, as in a group of people. Page 44.

ratio: proportional relation; a number or amount in relationship to another number or amount. For example, if a person spends ten hours inside and one hour outside the ratio is 10:1 or ten to one. Page 44.

rationalize: interpret or explain from a rational (reasonable) standpoint. Page 26.

raving: raging; delirious; frenzied and irrational. Page 94.

reactive: characterized by *reaction,* happening in (immediate) response to an influence; responding to an influence in a particular way or with particular behavior; "stimulus-response" type behavior. From Latin *reagere,* to do or act back. Page 13.

REACTIVE MIND: THAT PORTION OF THE MIND WHICH CONTAINS REFLEXIVE OR REACTIVE DATA WHICH DOES NOT CLEAR THROUGH THE ANALYTICAL MIND, BUT IS SUBJECT TO DRAMATIZATION OR ABERRATION. IT USES AS A THOUGHT PROCESS THE CONCEPTION OF IDENTITIES: A=A=A. THIS IS ESSENTIALLY THE ANIMAL THINKING MECHANISM. (From *LRH Glossary.*) Page 19.

rebuffed: bluntly and abruptly rejected, as a person's offer, approach or advance. Page 82.

recall(ed): bring back to mind; remember. Page 43.

recallable: that is able to be recalled. Page 45.

reception: the action or fact of receiving something. Page 42.

record(s): make a lasting account of facts or events; preserve the memory of something permanently, as in *"The physio-animal mind never ceases to be aware of now and never ceases to record the successive instances of now."* Page 19.

recount: tell of something verbally, giving the facts, details or particulars of an event or experience. Page 86.

reflexive: (of an action) performed without conscious thought. Page 114.

regress(ed): hypnotism used what was called "regression" on hypnotized subjects, the hypnotist sending the subject back to incidents in his past. This was done with trance techniques, drugs and considerable technology. It was a technique by which part of the individual's self remained in the present and part went back to the past. Page 45.

reiterated: said over again or repeatedly; repeated often or continually. Page 100.

release: literally, the action of unfixing something from some fastening or restraint. Also figuratively, relieving, lessening or removing the force or effect of. Page 44.

render: to cause to be or become; make. Page 115.

repercussion: an indirect or unforeseen effect of an act, action or event. Page 166.

repression(s): the action, process or result of suppressing into the unconscious or keeping out of the conscious mind unacceptable memories or desires. In Dianetics, a *repression* is an engramic command that the organism must not do something. Page 1.

reprimands: sharp criticisms of somebody for a wrongdoing. Page 70.

reserving: except for. Page 48.

reside: be located in a place or position. Page 113.

residual: present or existing. Page 36.

resigns: gives over or abandons something to a thing or condition. Page 165.

resilient: able to recover quickly, from illness, injury, mental pain, etc. Page 155.

resolve(d): 1. break up into separate elements or parts; analyze. Page 1.

2. deal with; find a solution to; cause to subside. Page 1.

3. find a solution or answer (to a problem); free from confusion or complication; solve. Page 10.

4. act as a solution, an answer or a means of settling a question or problem. Page 28.

respiration: the act of breathing air in and out. Page 18.

responsibilities: things which one is required to do as part of a job, role or life. Page 106.

responsive: not dull, apathetic or unaffected; reacting positively or favorably. Page 34.

RESTIMULATOR: THE ENVIRONMENTAL PERCEPTIC WHICH APPROXIMATES A PRECISE PART OF THE ENGRAMIC PERCEPTICS IN THE REACTIVE MIND. (From *LRH Glossary.*) Page 20.

retentive: having the power or capacity to hold or continue to hold something as for use, recognition, remembering or the like. Page 156.

retire: to go or fall back to. Page 26.

reverie: a light state of "concentration" not to be confused with hypnosis; in reverie the person is fully aware of what is taking place in the present. Page 85.

reversed polarity: that quality or condition in a physical body or system that manifests an opposite or contrasting property, as in a magnet where one end is positive and the other negative. One end is thought of as being reversed from what the other end is. Hence, *reversed polarity* refers to a state whereby one object, condition, etc., has an opposite characteristic, force, etc., to something else. Page 121.

reverses: changes from good fortune to bad; defeats. Page 67.

revivification: the action of reliving a past experience. *Reliving* occurs where a person is so thoroughly in the past for the moment that, while recalling an infant experience, if startled would react just as when a baby. Page 106.

rugged: strong; sturdy. Page 72.

sag: lower in tone. Page 104.

save: except, but. Page 72.

scanner(s): a device that passes a beam across a screen in order to display an image. *See also* **scanning mechanism.** Page 40.

scanning mechanism: literally, a device used in some electronic equipment to display pictures. The *scanning mechanism,* a special gun and system for focusing and changing angle, is located at one end of a glass tube. The gun sends off a beam of minute electronically charged particles (electrons) to a screen coated with a chemical that produces a fluorescent glow where the electrons strike. As the beam rapidly scans or sweeps across the entire screen with varying intensity, images are formed on the screen. Used to describe something similar in the mind. Page 96.

school: a body of persons that has been taught by or follows a particular authority or teacher and is associated or united by common principles, beliefs, methods, etc. Page 7.

science: knowledge; comprehension or understanding of facts or principles, classified and made available in work, life or the search for truth. A science is a connected body of demonstrated truths or observed facts systematically organized and bound together under general laws. It includes trustworthy methods for the discovery of new truth within its domain and denotes the application of scientific methods in fields of study previously considered open only to theories based on subjective, historical or undemonstrable, abstract criteria. The word *science* is used in this sense—the most fundamental meaning and tradition of the word—and not in the sense of the *physical* or *material* sciences. Page 7.

scrutiny: a searching study or inquiry; close inspection; examination. Page 85.

seat: a place in which something occurs or is established; location. Page 113.

second-grade: a degree or step in a scale that is somewhat low as to quality, value or quantity. For instance, first-grade would be the best or most of something, second-grade would be less and third-grade would be thought of as much less. Page 10.

select: chosen out of a larger group on account of suitability, preference, etc., as for a particular purpose. Page vii.

self-control: *self-hypnosis,* the act or process of hypnotizing oneself; also, a self-induced hypnotic state or condition. Page 70.

semantic: of, pertaining to or arising from the different meanings of words or other symbols; of or relating to meaning in language. Page 7.

semantics: generally, the study or science of meaning in language forms such as the meaning of a word, phrase, sentence or text. More specifically, a reference to *general semantics,* a highly organized philosophical approach to language, developed by Alfred Korzybski (1879–1950), which sought a scientific basis for a clear understanding of the difference between words and what words represent in the real world as well as the ways in which words themselves can influence and limit Man's ability to think. He developed a system of the different categories of perceptions (called sensations) and created a precise table displaying their various physical characteristics and properties. Page 39.

semblance: the slightest appearance or amount of (something). Page 110.

sensibilities: a person's moral, emotional or aesthetic ideas, feelings or standards, especially how readily he might take offense in regard to them. Page 81.

sensitive: highly perceptive or responsive intellectually, aesthetically, etc.; highly responsive to external conditions. Page 20.

sensory: of or pertaining to the senses or sensation such as sight, hearing, touch, smell. Page 39.

sensory strip: a long, narrow area of the brain which is believed to monitor the senses of the body such as sight, smell, touch and hearing. *Sensory* means connected with the reception and transmission of sense impressions. Page 88.

sentient: conscious or capable of perceptions; consciously perceiving. Page 160.

serviceable: that can be of service; ready for use; useful. Page 72.

shadow: 1. in psychology, the dark aspect of personality formed by those fears and unpleasant emotions that are rejected by a person but which exist in the unconscious, as in *"It can be called a 'shadow mind,' instantaneously reactive when any of its content is perceived in the environment of the individual."* Page 20.

2. anything unsubstantial (not solid or factual) or unreal, though having the deceptive appearance of reality, as in *"These are shadow things."* Page 118.

shadowy: of or characteristic of something which is an unreal appearance or an unsubstantial (not solid or factual) object; of an indistinct image. Page 72.

shock wave: a sudden increase in the amount of electrical energy traveling along the nerves, caused by a *shock,* a sudden and violent forcible impact. Page 115.

short, in: introducing a summary statement of what has been previously stated in a few words; in summary. Page 34.

shunned: avoided deliberately and intentionally. Page 69.

significance(s): the meaning of something. Page 40.

simulate: imitate the character, conditions or appearance of. Page 116.

slap of the cable: a reference to the sound made by the belts (cables) of a dentist's rotating drill. The drill was connected to a motor through a series of belts that sometimes made a slapping sound against the metal arm to which they were affixed. Page 44.

slumber: be in a state of inactivity. Page 118.

so as to: a phrase used to show a result; in order to; as a means to, as in *"When the human being in the womb is injured, his senses extend so as to record sounds outside the mother's body."* Page 156.

sociological: dealing with social questions or problems, especially focusing on cultural and environmental factors rather than on personal (mental) characteristics. Page 48.

so far as: to the degree or extent. Page 8.

soldered: fastened with *solder,* any of various metals that melt at low temperatures and which when heated will flow into a joint between metal parts to unite them. *Soldering* is used in electronics to firmly unite two parts so that electricity will flow between them. Hence, joined, fastened or cemented (to something). Page 118.

so long as: under the condition that; provided that. Page 20.

SOMATIC: THE PHYSIOLOGICAL COUNTERPART OF MENTAL ABERRATION. A SOMATIC ATTENDS EVERY ABERRATION. THIS TERM IS USED IN LIEU OF "PHYSICAL PAIN" IN THERAPY, DUE TO THE HIGH ENGRAMIC VALUE OF THE WORD "PAIN" AND ITS FAILURE TO INCLUDE IN ITS MEANING ALL PAINFUL PERCEPTICS. (From *LRH Glossary.*) From Greek *somatikos,* pertaining to the body. A somatic is a pain, body sensation or psychosomatic illness experienced when contacting an engram or when an engram is restimulated, the pain or psychosomatic illness is the re-experiencing of the content of the engram. Page 44.

somatically: by means of a somatic. The auditor observes a somatic in the individual, inquires about it and uses the data to locate the area of the engram. Page 45.

somnambulistic: of the nature of sleepwalking or the performance of other acts while asleep, specifically when the actions are not recalled after waking. Page 19.

spaces: places or arranges at definite intervals or distances. Page 68.

specializing: adapting (parts, organs, etc.) to a special use, requirement or environment. Page 8.

species: 1. a group or class of animals or plants having certain common and permanent characteristics which clearly distinguish it from other groups and which can breed with one another, such as tigers, rabbits and squirrels. Page 8.
2. a distinct kind, variety or type. Page 166.

species, the: the human race. Page 27.

spiritualism: the doctrine or belief that the spirits of the dead can and do communicate with the living, especially through a person (medium). Page 8.

sporadic: happening from time to time; not constant or regular, occasional. Page 53.

static: fixed, stationary; not changing. Page 174.

stimuli: plural of *stimulus,* any action or agent that causes or changes an activity in an organism, organ or part, as something that starts a nerve impulse, activates a muscle, etc. Page 113.

stirring: prompting to action, as from an indifferent or quiet state. Page 81.

stream of electrons: a flow of minute electronically charged particles. Page 107.

strip, motor: a long narrow area of the brain, which is believed to control the movement of the various muscles and movements of the body. *Motor* means of, relating to, or being a nerve that passes from the central nervous system to a muscle, conducting an impulse that causes movement. Page 88.

strip, sensory: a long narrow area of the brain, which is believed to monitor the senses of the body such as sight, smell, touch and hearing. *Sensory* means connected with the reception and transmission of sense impressions. Page 88.

sub-brains: various nerve centers in the body such as the elbow, knee, inside of the wrist, etc. Page 18.

subconscious: *(psychology)* existing or operating in the mind but not immediately available to consciousness; affecting thought, feeling and behavior without entering awareness. Page 22.

succeeding: coming next after something else; following. Page 45.

successive: happening or existing one after another. Page 19.

suggestion(s): the action of prompting one to a particular action or course of action; the putting into the mind of an idea, an object or thought. Specifically in hypnosis, the process of influencing a person to accept an idea, command, impulse, etc., without his conscious knowledge. Page 43.

suggestion, positive: in hypnosis, a suggestion or command which is given to a hypnotized subject who then obeys it unknowingly. Also, any phrase or command in the mind acting like one given to a hypnotized person. For example: A man is placed in a hypnotic trance by standard hypnotic technique or some hypnotic drug. The operator then may say to him, "When you awaken, there is something you must do. Whenever I touch my tie, you will remove your coat. When I let go of my tie, you will put on your coat. Now you will forget that I have told you to do this." The subject is then awakened. He is not consciously aware of the command. If told he had been given an order while "asleep," he would resist the idea or shrug, but he would not know. The operator then touches his tie. The subject may make some remark about its being too warm and so take his coat off. The operator then releases his tie. The subject may remark that he is now cold and will put his coat back on. See *Dianetics: The Modern Science of Mental Health*. Page 43.

superimposed: imposed or placed on or upon another; laid above or on the top. *Super-* means over, above or on and *impose* means to place on or onto. Page 11.

supplants: causes to fall from a position of power; uproots; brings low. Page 40.

surcharge: an additional or excessive charge, load or supply of electricity or energy. In Dianetics it refers to an excessive amount of harmful energy in the mind, as in *"An engram is an apparent surcharge in the mental circuit with certain definite, finite content."* Page 43.

suspension: a state of being (temporarily) stopped or made ineffective; interruption. Page 54.

sustenance: nourishment that supports life; food. Page 156.

sweep (over): pass along or across something with a steady, continuous motion. Page 40.

syllabic: consisting of *syllables,* words or parts of words pronounced with a single, uninterrupted sounding of the voice. Page 39.

symbiote(s): the Dianetic meaning of *symbiote* is extended beyond the dictionary definition, "the living together of two dissimilar organisms," to mean any or all life or energy forms which are mutually dependent for survival. The atom depends on the universe, the universe on the atom. Page 9.

symptomatic: that is a symptom or sign of something; serving as a symptom or sign of a condition, quality, etc.; characteristic and indicative of. Page 107.

tactile: the sense of touch. Page 39.

taken into account: considered along with other factors before observing something, reaching a decision or taking action. Page 97.

tangled: twisted into a confused mass, as of strands, threads or the like so as to be very difficult to unravel. Page 181.

tantrums: outbursts of anger or frustration, especially childish displays of rage or bad temper. Page 68.

telegraphically: in the manner of a message sent by *telegraph,* a method of long-distance communication originally conveying written words as coded electric impulses transmitted through wires. Charges for such messages were based on the number of words in the message and hence, the text was usually very concise. Page 114.

telepathy: supposed communication directly from one person's mind to another's without speech, writing or other signs or symbols. Page 8.

tenacity: the quality or property of being *tenacious,* persistently continuing, keeping a firm hold on; toughness. Page 11.

tenet: any opinion, principle, doctrine, belief, etc., especially one held true by members of a profession, group or movement. Page 106.

tentatively: in a manner that is not fully concluded. Page 180.

therapeutic: of or having to do with *therapy,* the administration and application of Dianetics techniques and procedures to resolve problems concerning human behavior and psychosomatic illness. Page 40.

therapy: the administration and application of Dianetics techniques and procedures to resolve problems concerning human behavior and psychosomatic illness. Page 28.

thesis: a systematic spoken or written treatment of a subject which includes results of original research and establishes by proof or evidence the existence or truth of specific phenomena. Page vii.

the species: the human race. Page 27.

third-grade: a degree or step in a scale that is low as to quality, value or quantity. For instance, first-grade would be the best or most of something, second-grade would be less and third-grade would be thought of as much less. Page 10.

thought: 1. a single act or product of thinking; an item of mental activity; something that one thinks or has thought; a thing that is in the mind; an idea, notion, etc., as in a *"science of thought."* Page 7. **2.** the action or process of thinking; mental action or activity in general, especially that of the intellect; exercise of the mental faculty; formation and arrangement of ideas in the mind, as in *"The field of thought may be divided into two areas"* or *"solely reactive thought"* or *"three kinds of* thought.*"* Page 7.

3. the intellectual activity or mental product characteristic of the thinkers of a particular class, time or place; what is or has been thought by the philosophers or learned men of some specified country, etc., as in *"the thinker of the New Thought."* Page 10.

Thought, New: literally, any of various philosophical and religious movements such as the New Thought movement (late 1800s) and its offshoots, holding that affirmative thought or the adoption of a favorable mental attitude results in beneficial changes in Man. Their workable optimism was in contrast with the "old thought" of sin, evil and pessimistic resignation. Hence, *"the thinker of the New Thought,"* an individual or group that brings new, independent and constructive philosophic or religious insight or principles to Mankind. Page 10.

three kingdoms: three broad divisions of natural objects: the animal, vegetable and mineral kingdoms. A *kingdom* is a region or sphere of nature. Page 13.

thrust: 1. a (forceful or otherwise) movement in a usually specified direction; a driving, vital, energetic force thought of as moving forward, as in *"the dynamic thrust into time and space of an individual, a species, or a unit of matter or energy."* Page 11.

2. forced into a specified condition or situation, as in *"since it was thrust, without his consent."* Page 70.

timbre: the character, quality, color or tone of a voice or instrument, distinct from such things as its volume. It is the timbre that distinguishes one voice from another or one musical instrument from another, as when two instruments play the same note (and sound different). Page 39.

time after time: again and again; repeatedly. Page 104.

TIME TRACK: THE MEMORY RECORD OF AN INDIVIDUAL, MOTOR OR SENSORY, IS PRECISELY ALIGNED ON MOMENTS OF TIME. IN A CLEAR, ALL SUCH MOMENTS ARE AVAILABLE TO THE ANALYTICAL MIND. IN AN ABERREE, AREAS OF THE TIME TRACK ARE OBSCURED, BUT THE TIME TRACK IS CONSIDERED TO BE IN

PERFECT CONDITION, IF PARTIALLY AND TEMPORARILY OBSCURED. THE EXISTENCE OF TWO TIME TRACKS IS SUSPECTED—ONE SENSORY AND ONE MOTOR, THE LATTER BEING MORE AVAILABLE TO THE AUDITOR IN THE FORM OF SOMATICS. THE TIME TRACK IS PRECISE, BUT AS THE ANALYTICAL MIND ADDRESSES IT IN THE ABERREE IT IS APPARENTLY OBLITERATED IN PART OR TANGLED. (From *LRH Glossary.*) Page 19.

TONE: THE EMOTIONAL CONDITION OF AN ENGRAM OR THE GENERAL CONDITION OF AN INDIVIDUAL. (From *LRH Glossary.*) Page 48.

Tone 4: the term *Tone 4* denotes an engram or a preclear who has achieved complete rationality and cheerfulness. Page 60.

touched upon: mentioned or dealt with in a brief way, as in the course of discussion. Page 17.

trance: place in or as if in a *trance,* a semiconscious state, as between sleeping and waking. Page 45.

tranquillity: the quality or state of being quiet, calm and peaceful. Page 108.

TRAUMA: A TERM FROM A SCHOOL OF PSYCHOLOGY IMPLYING AN EXPERIENCE WHICH WOULD CREATE A PSYCHIC SCAR. IT IS UNUSED IN DIANETICS AS BEING LIABLE TO MISUNDERSTANDING OF THE NATURE OF SEVERE EXPERIENCES. SCARS CANNOT BE REMOVED; PSYCHOSOMATIC EXPERIENCES CAN BE. (From *LRH Glossary.*)

treatment: the practice of Dianetics techniques and procedures to resolve problems concerning human behavior and psychosomatic illness. Page 28.

trite: lacking in freshness or effectiveness because of constant use or excessive repetition. Page 89.

Truth: ideal or fundamental reality apart from and transcending perceived experience. Page 7.

ulcers: open sores (other than a wound) on the skin or some internal organ, as the lining of the stomach, characterized by the disintegration of the affected tissue. Page 1.

UNCONSCIOUSNESS: A PERIOD OF CESSATION OF ACTIVITY ON THE PART OF THE ANALYTICAL MIND ONLY. THE REACTIVE MIND IS ACTIVE AND IS CONSCIOUS IN THE MAJORITY OF HIS BEING, IN ALL DEGREES OF LIFE, NO MATTER HOW NEARLY APPROACHING DEATH.

(THIS IS A CONDITION OF THE TOTAL INDIVIDUAL IN DEATH ONLY.) (From *LRH Glossary.*) Page 19.

unhampered: allowed to act, move or progress freely. Page 151.

uniformly: consistently; without variation or alteration; invariably. Page 17.

unit form, in: in the shape or arrangement of a *unit,* something which is single and complete or operates as an independent whole. Page 10.

unity: something which is complete, whole or entire in itself. Page 7.

unreasoned: done without judgment; lacking rational or logical sense. Page 148.

unstack: literally, remove, take down from being stacked or piled (one by one). Used figuratively. Page 158.

unwitting: unaware of what is happening in a particular situation. Page 171.

upon: used to indicate that one event is followed immediately by another event, as in *"vanish upon the removal of the engram from the reactive mind."* Page 45.

usurped: taken the place of by or as if by force. Page 113.

utterance: vocal expression; manner of speaking. Page 39.

value: meaning, force or significance. Page 45.

vanish: the words *vanished* or *erased,* when applied to an engram which has been treated, mean that the engram has disappeared from the engram bank. It cannot be found afterwards except by search of the standard memory. Page 43.

verbatim: word for word; in exactly the same words. Page 172.

vices: evil or wicked actions, habits or characteristics; evil or wicked conduct or behavior. Page 34.

victimized: caused to be a *victim,* one who is harmed by or made to suffer from an act, circumstance or condition. Page 46.

virtues: general moral excellence; right actions and thinking; goodnesses or moralities. Page 34.

visio: having to do with the sense of sight. Page 39.

vocational therapies: *vocational* means relating to education designed to provide the necessary skills for a particular job or career.

Vocational therapy is the preparation and placement of those with some sort of mental difficulty (from mild to severe) in a job where they can be successful. Also referred to as *work therapy*. Page 106.

voluntary muscles: muscles that are normally controlled by or subject to the individual's conscious choice, such as the muscles responsible for moving one's arm. Page 18.

warp: turn from the true, natural or right condition, course or direction; twist or distort. Page 106.

way, in some: in an unspecified manner; somehow. Page 108.

whereas: in contrast or comparison with the fact that; taking into consideration the fact that. Page 122.

wherein: in what or in which (place, thing, condition, matter, action, etc.); in, at, during or in the course of which. Page 19.

which is to say: a phrase used to introduce a clearer, more comprehensible restatement of what immediately precedes or to limit or modify it. Page 20.

willpower: strength of will, mind or determination; self-control. Page 34.

wise: way or manner. Page 127.

without: outside of; exterior to. Page 10.

wittingly: knowingly; consciously. Page 150.

words, in other: put differently; otherwise stated, often used to introduce an explanation of something and usually in a simpler way. Page 26.

work(s): 1. all things made, established or created as a result of effort, activity, labor and so forth. *"All works and energies can be considered to be motivated by it."* Page 8.

2. the action of executing or performing an action with or upon something, such as auditing an engram, as in *"The* Tone Scale *denotes numerically, first, the status of an engram in the reactive mind, next, its progress during work."* Page 59.

3. manage; solve by calculation and reasoning, as in *"There are five ways in which it* [the analytical mind] *can work solutions about that pain."* Page 115.

4. make function or operate, as in *"since it* [the analytical mind] *must work not only a mind, but the entire organism and the entities and energy forms included in its dynamics."* Page 121.

work, at: in operation; having an effect on something. Page 108.

worked: 1. executed effectively; made to function or operate as intended, as in *"Dianetics will work, and can only be worked, when regarded and used as a unity."* Page 7.

2. executed or performed an action with or upon something, as in, *"Once an auditor has worked a* prenatal engram *and has seen its influence upon the engram chain and the awake life of the adult, no question will remain in his mind concerning the actuality of the experience."* Page 47.

working: 1. active; accomplishing what is desired; effective, as in *"As this is apparently the most workable solution, natural selection best preserves those species which follow this working rule."* Page 10.

2. that which is needed for continued practical use and application, as in *"This is a necessary part of an auditor's working knowledge."* Page 34.

zealot: a person who shows excessive enthusiasm for a cause, particularly a religious cause. Page 150.

Index

A

AA

  definition, 182

  see also **attempted abortion**

A=A=A

  engramic thinking and, 66

  reactive mind and, 114

aberrated personality, 128

  sympathy engram and, 95

  see also **aberree (aberrated individual)**

aberration, 53–56

  absence of analytical power and, 18

  actual personality versus, 155

  after five years old and, 162

  analytical mind and, 117

  antipathies and, 70

  basic individual and, 27

  become people at will without, 95

  child raised by parents with, 107

  Clear, aberrated spouse and, 108

  contagion of, 108–110, 115

  curing human mind's, 7

  definition, 165

  demonstrating one's, 43

  Dianetics and, 7, 17

  dramatization and, 147

  dynamics and society's, 26

  dynamic strength lessened by, 36

  educational versus aberrational information, 156

  engramic commands and, 53

  engrams and, 70

    general rule, 165

    occasioning all, 47

    precise content of, 66

    severity of, 44

  example, 56

  holding hard to, 36

  holding on to, 73

    engram chain and, 130

  inability to conceive differences, and, 54

  justified thought and, 42

  justifying, 73

  mild, 148

  physical, 56

  rational being versus, 94

  reactive mind and, 22

  self-determinism versus, 34

  sociological maladjustments, parental punishments and, 48

  somatic aberration locating, 88

  somatics and, 44

  time and, 171

  unconscious moments and, 69

aberree (aberrated individual), 182

  conduct of, 150

dramatization and, 147, 148
engrams and, 36
exterior observation and, 127
fixed person and, 94
more than one engram chain
found in, 139
personalities and, 128
post-birth, 158
willpower and, 151

ability
neurosis and inhibited, 56

Abnormal Dianetics, 106
definition, 179
description, 18
purpose, 13, 17
testing and results of, 1

abortion
attempted, *see* **attempted
abortion**
parents dramatizing and, 159

abyss
of irrational, solely reactive
thought, 13

action
reactive mind and errors in, 20

affinity
attempting to survive in, 13
auditor, preclear and, 81, 82
Dianetic auditing and, 151
survival factor and, 25

allergies, 79, 160
Dianetics successfully
resolving, 1

alleviation, 151
description, 141
treatment of locks and, 143

amentia, 54, 106

amnesia-tranced patient, 43

analytical mind, 68, 113–123, 129,
169
aberration of, 17

auditor
as preclear's additional, 93
preclear and, 79
auditor's
and preclear's, 85
understanding of, 113
automatic computer, 118
basic purpose and, 122
Clear and, 129
intelligence, 122
conception to birth and, 156
data and solving problems, 105
definition, 183
denial of engrams to, 166
description, 20, 113, 114
difficulties encountered when
returned, 172
dispersal
not operating and, 50
of awareness of, 69
of thought process of, 22
efforts to rationalize and, 46
engrams and, 42, 53
receipt of, 173
unavailable to, 65
evolving solution and, 116
experience and educational
data, 156
good in intent, 118
high awareness and, 148
"I" and, 127
in complete command of
organism, 72
injury, illness supplanting, 40
insanity and, 150
integrated being and, 128
itself, incapable of error, 121
justification and, 66
justified thought and, 42, 44
less and less powerful, 67
locks more or less known
to, 139
multiple scanners, 40

F

failure
    justified thought and, 42
    mind directing organism to
      avoid, 9

faith healing phenomena, 166

false data
    Clear and, 122
    engrams and, 139
      exhausting from, 118, 119

false purpose
    assist engram and, 150
    establishment of, 106

family
    aiding, 13
    combination of dynamics, 27
    insanity running in, 107
    preclear's, auditor and, 108
    source of difficulty in, 108

fear, 156
    Clear untroubled by
      aberrated, 132
    extended range of perception
      and, 156
    of dark, attempted abortion
      and, 157

fetus
    dropping word from
      language, 157
    painful experience and, 47
    perceptics of, 48
    prenatal engrams and, 97

finite universe
    Dynamic Principle of
      Existence and, 8

fixed person, 94

flee
    danger and, 67
    source of pain and, 167

floater
    definition, 45
    engrams, locks and, 46
    example of, 46

fluids (body), 115
    mind and, 47
    physio-animal mind and, 18

follower, 96
    not permitting data to rise, 104

forgetter mechanisms, 69

fuse mechanism (system)
    analytical mind and, 22, 115, 131

G

geometrical progression
    awareness potential, 147

glands, 66
    commands to, 68
    glandular
      condition, 33
      readjustment, 56

goal
    aberrated conduct threatening
      one's, 18
    auditor's first, 142
    basic personality and, 69
    individual man's, 13
    infinite, 25
    mind directing organism to
      accomplish, 9
    ultimate, 9
      Dianetics and, 13

Go back to the time when
    _____, 86

good
    definition, 13

gradation
    eternal survival, death and, 9

group
    aiding, 13

responsibility, 70

restimulation
assist engram and, 150
auditor's own, 79
child and, 107
chronic, 53, 131
state of, 66
dramatization and, 147
physical pain and, 151
engrams subject to, 156
floaters, chronics and, 45
perceptics in engram and, 118
reactive mind and, 22
reduction of awareness
and, 148

restimulator
aberrations and, 43
aberrees and, 148
analytical mind and, 117
associative, 183
auditor and, 171
birth and asthma, 160
child and mother, 46, 107
chronic, 94
codified restimulator list, 88
definition, 20, 42, 182
dramatization and, 66, 148
engrams and, 42
perception of engram's, 66
removal of individual from, 46
routing direct to reactive
mind, 68
timelessness and, 54
tone of person and, 60

results
Dianetics and
achieving best, 69
predictable, 7
100 percent, 168

returning, 165–175
definition and description, 86
difficulties with, 173

inability in, 93
many times to incident, 103
period of pain and, 97
preclear's behavior in, 172
reactive mind removed by, 85
wide awake and, 86

reverie, 169
canceller and, 86
description, 85

reversal of charge, 129

"reverse charge," 40

revivification, 88, 151
Dianetic, 106

run
danger and, 67
see also **flee**

S

sag, 105
assist engram and, 150
basic engram and
description, 141
test for, 174
engram lifting without
laughter and, 104
Tone 4 and, 104

sanity
eradicate pain and return, 69
Tone Scale and measure of, 59

scale
from death to immortality, 9

scanners
engrams unavailable to
conscious, 49
forcing to contact engramic
data, 96
multiple
analytical mind and, 40
locks being reached by, 45
purpose, 96

Your Next Book

Why is Dianetics the best-selling self-help book of all time?

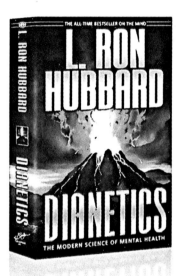

The answer is
CLEAR

The Reactive Mind underlies and enslaves Man. It's the source of your nightmares, unreasonable fears, upsets and insecurity. And now you can get rid of it. For here is the complete handbook of Dianetics Procedure and the means to achieve the State of Clear. It's been a bestseller for more than five decades. And with tens of millions of copies in circulation, it's generated a movement across every continent of Earth. Here is the bolt from the blue that started it all. And that is why it will forever be known as *Book One*.

DIANETICS
THE MODERN SCIENCE OF MENTAL HEALTH

Available from any Church of Scientology or direct from the publisher
www.bridgepub.com • www.newerapublications.com